EMPLOYMEI

C000108773

Colin Thomas, LLB(Hons.), Dip. Ed., is a Barrister and Senior Lecturer in Law at Liverpool Polytechnic. He specialises in company law and labour law, and is the author of *Company Law*, also published in the Teach Yourself series.

TEACH YOURSELF BOOKS

To Rita

EMPLOYMENT LAW

Colin Thomas

TEACH YOURSELF BOOKS

Hodder and Stoughton

First published 1984

Copyright © 1984
Colin Thomas

All rights reserved. No part of this publication may be
reproduced or transmitted in any form or by any means,
electronic or mechanical, including photocopy, recording,
or any information storage and retrieval system, without
permission in writing from the publisher.

British Library Cataloguing in Publication Data

Thomas, Colin
    Employment law.—(Teach yourself books)
    1. Labor laws and legislation—Great Britain
    I. Title
    344.104'1125   KD3009

    ISBN 0 340 35621 9

Printed and bound in Great Britain for
Hodder and Stoughton Educational,
a division of Hodder and Stoughton Ltd,
Mill Road, Dunton Green, Sevenoaks, Kent,
by Hazell, Watson & Viney Ltd,
Aylesbury, Buckinghamshire
Photoset by Rowland Phototypesetting Ltd,
Bury St Edmunds, Suffolk.

Contents

Work Act 1974. Duties imposed by the HSWA. Enforcement of the HSWA.

Abbreviations

EA 1980	Employment Act 1980
EA 1982	Employment Act 1982
EPA 1975	Employment Protection Act 1975
EPCA	Employment Protection (Consolidation) Act 1978
HSWA	Health and Safety at Work Act 1974
RRA	Race Relations Act 1976
SDA	Sex Discrimination Act 1975
SSA	Social Security Act 1975
TULRA	Trade Union and Labour Relations Act 1974
EAT	Employment Appeal Tribunal

Preface

This book provides an outline of the basic rights and duties of the parties to a contract of employment. As such, it will appeal to students, trade unionists, personnel managers, and anyone concerned with the fields of employment and industrial relations.

All information contained in this book is believed to have been correct at the time of going to press. The main difficulty in writing the book was in deciding which cases to include from the ever-changing mass of case law decided by the courts and tribunals.

I am grateful to my daughter Catherine for undertaking research in certain topics in the employment field, and to my students over the years who have made lecturing in this subject such a pleasant task. I should also like to thank *Employment News* for permission to reproduce the summary of the Employment Act 1982.

References in the text to male employees apply equally to female employees, with a few specified exceptions.

Colin Thomas

1

The Contract of Employment

Employment legislation has in the last decade dealt comprehensively with the rights and obligations of the parties to contracts of employment. Employees' rights have been the subject of a number of Acts, and the Employment Protection (Consolidation) Act 1978 consolidates 'certain enactments relating to the rights of employees arising out of their employment'.

It is therefore important to determine whether a person is an employee for the following reasons:

1   Only employees and apprentices are entitled to the various benefits conferred by the EPCA, for example, redundancy payments, compensation for unfair dismissal, and so on.
2   There are different rates of national insurance contributions for employees and for self-employed persons. The benefits also differ, for example, self-employed persons are not entitled to industrial injury or unemployment benefits.
3   Income tax is generally deducted from an employee's wages under the PAYE system. Self-employed persons are subject to direct tax assessments under a different schedule of the Income Tax Acts.
4   An employer owes a greater duty of care to his employee than to other individuals. Although he owes a common duty of care (under the Occupiers Liability Act) to any visitor who enters his property, he owes a particular duty under both the common law and the Health and Safety at Work Act to provide for the safety and welfare of his employees.

5   An employer is vicariously liable for the torts (civil wrongs) committed by his employees in the course of employment.

6   There are various obligations owed by the employer to the employees, and vice versa, which do not arise unless there is a contract of employment. These rights and obligations are dealt with in detail in Chapters 3 and 4.

Although various Acts refer to the contract of employment, they do not attempt to define such a contact. The courts have therefore formulated various tests and guidelines to determine whether a contract of employment (otherwise known as a *contract of service*) exists in a given situation.

As Lord Denning once remarked: 'It is often easy to recognise a *contract of service* when you see it, but difficult to say wherein the difference lies'.

There are other contractual relationships in which one party renders service to another which are not contracts of service. The most common example is that of a person who enters into a contract with another to undertake a specific task, e.g. if I ask an electrician to fit an additional power socket in my garage. A contract comes into existence, but it is a *contract for services*, as opposed to *a contract of service*. The electrician is an independent contractor, and I am not his employer.

Webster J. in *WHPT Association v. Social Services Secretary* observed that '. . . the difference between a contract of service and one for services must reside, essentially in the terms of the principal obligation agreed to be undertaken by the employee . . . In a contract of service, it seems to me, the principal obligation undertaken by the employee is to provide himself to serve: whereas in a contract for services the principal obligation is not to provide himself to serve the employer, but his services for the use of the employer'.

Tests to determine employee status

Three tests have been formulated by the courts, namely: *(a)* the control test; *(b)* the organisation test; and *(c)* the multiple test.

Control test

Over a century ago Bramwell B stated that 'a servant is a person subject to the command of his master as to the manner in which he shall do his work'.

The essence of the control test is an employer's right to control what an employee does, how he does it, and when and where the work should be done. An employer thus exercises control over the nature of the work, the manner of its performance, and the time and place of accomplishment.

In *Short v. Henderson*, it was stated that there are four indicia of a contract of service:

1 The employer's power of selection of his employee;
2 The payment of wages or other remuneration;
3 The employer's right to control the method of doing the work;
4 The employer's right of suspension or dismissal.

The operation of the test can be shown in its application in two cases. In *Midland Sinfonia Concert Society Ltd v. Secretary of State for Social Services*, the Society engaged musicians to play in its orchestra by invitation at irregular intervals. The musicians were paid solely in respect of the occasions when they played, and income tax was not deducted from these payments. It was held that the company's control over the musicians was minimal, in that they assembled as an orchestra to fulfill an engagement and the control exercised by the conductor during the performance of a concert was a fundamental part of orchestral playing. There was no control which could amount to control of the musicians as to the manner in which they carried out their work. They were therefore not employees of the Society.

In *Hawley v. Fieldcastle and Co. Ltd*, the applicant sued for unfair dismissal after working with Fieldcastle and Co. Ltd under a work experience programme, sponsored by the Manpower Services Commission. He was entitled to claim if he could show that an employee/employer relationship existed. The industrial tribunal held that as the Manpower Services Commission imposed some restriction on the parties in the five principal components of the normal employment relationship, a contract of employment did not exist. The five principal components listed were as follows: recruitment, the work to be done, discipline, the ending of the relationship, and remuneration.

The control test, although still of importance, has become an unreliable exclusive test in an ever-changing industrial society. It is unsatisfactory in cases where the traditional test of employer's control cannot be applied, for example, a captain of an aircraft or a hospital doctor.

Other tests have therefore been formulated, as it is now accepted that the degree of control exercised by an employer is no longer the decisive factor in determining the existence of a contract of employment.

Organisation or integration test
This test was formulated in response to the limitations of the control test. Lord Denning in his Hamlyn Lectures stated 'I would observe the test of being a servant does not rest nowadays on submission to orders. It depends on whether the person is part and parcel of the organisation'.

In *Cassidy v. Ministry of Heath*, a patient sued a hospital for post-operative negligence by its doctors, as a result of which he lost the use of his hand. It was held that the hospital authorities were liable, despite the fact that they were unable to exercise real control over the work performed by those doctors who were employed by them, as the patient had entrusted himself to the care of an organisation.

In *Morren v. Swinton and Pendlebury Borough Council*, a local authority engaged a resident engineer to supervise the construction of a sewage works. He worked under the instructions of a consultant engineer, who was retained by the authority. The local authority paid his salary, national insurance contributions, holiday pay and subsistence allowances. They also reserved the right to dismiss him. It was held that he was an employee as there was a sufficient degree of integration into the organisation, despite the absence of control as to the manner in which he carried out his work.

The organisation test has not received widespread support, partly due to the difficulty in defining 'integration' and 'organisation'. This has led to the development of the multiple test.

Multiple test

This test examines the economic reality and the totality of a relationship before arriving at a conclusion. In *Ready Mixed Concrete (South East) Ltd v. Minister of Pensions and National Insurance*, McKenna J. stated that he considered that a contract of service existed if the following three conditions were fulfilled:

1 The servant agrees that in consideration of a wage or other remuneration he will provide his own work and skill in the performance of some service for his master.
2 He agrees, expressly or implicitly, that in the performance of that service he will be subject to the other's control in a sufficient degree to make that other master (control includes the power of deciding the thing to be done, the way in which it shall be done, the means to be employed in doing it, the time when, and the place where it shall be done).
3 The other provisions of the contract are consistent with it being a contract of service.

The first two conditions listed are self-explanatory. The third allows the courts a degree of latitude to balance each factor and arrive at a conclusion based on all the terms of the contract.

In the *Ready Mixed Concrete* case above, the driver of a ready mixed concrete lorry bought the lorry on hire purchase by arrangement with the company. He was required to wear the company's livery, obey reasonable orders from the company's servants, maintain the lorry, and use it solely for the company's business. He was paid a mileage rate for work undertaken for the company. The court held that he was not an employee as he operated the vehicle at his own risk, having to meet the expenses and depend upon the mileage rate paid by the company for his livelihood.

The operation of this test can best be illustrated by the following cases. In *Ferguson v. John Dawson Ltd*, a builder's labourer worked on the 'lump' i.e. according to a practice in the building industry where a contractor is paid a lump sum to provide labour to complete a job. Such workers are regarded as self-employed. John Dawson Ltd did not make any deductions from Ferguson's pay in respect of income tax or national insurance contributions, and until Ferguson was injured the parties regarded the plaintiff's status as that of an independent contractor. Ferguson was injured as a result of John

Dawson Ltd's failure to provide a guard rail on a flat roof, and was entitled to damages if he could prove that his status was that of an employee. The court held that, despite the label put on the contract by the parties, 'in reality the contract . . . was a contract of service', as John Dawson Ltd's agent was responsible for 'hiring and firing,' moving the workforce from site to site, providing the necessary tools and telling the workmen what particular work they were to do. Ferguson was entitled to damages of £30 000.

In *Massey v. Crown Life Insurance Company*, the plaintiff attempted to claim for unfair dismissal, after electing to become self-employed. Although his duties as a Branch Manager remained unchanged, he was taxed under Schedule D and paid his own national insurance contributions. It was held that he was self-employed as he had acted on the advice of his accountant and of his own volition. All the indicia were evenly balanced, and as he had elected to become self-employed, he was not entitled to bring a claim for unfair dismissal for he was no longer an employee.

In *Young and Woods v. West Ltd*, a sheet metal worker at West's factory chose to be treated as a self-employed person. No deductions were made from his pay for tax or national insurance contributions. He did not receive any holiday pay or sickness benefit from the company. He later complained of unfair dismissal. The Court of Appeal asked the question 'Is the person who has engaged himself to perform those services performing them as a person in business on his own account?' It held that it would be impossible to regard Young in this light. He was therefore an employee, and entitled to the protection afforded to employees. This case may be distinguished from the previous case in that there was a deliberate change of relationship in Massey's case, and Massey originally had two contracts – under a general agency agreement and under a contract of employment.

However, in *Davies v. New England College of Arundel*, a professional freelance lecturer was held to be employed under a contract of service, despite the parties' agreement that he should be regarded as self-employed. The reality of the situation was that his employment was clearly under the control of the defendants as his contract was similar to those of the other members of staff who were employed by the defendants. He was therefore entitled to bring a claim for unfair dismissal.

In *Hitchcock v. Post Office*, a sub-postmaster contended that he was a Post Office employee, as the Post Office exercised a degree of control over Post Office business. It was held that as Hitchcock provided premises and part of the equipment at his own expense and also engaged employees, he was carrying on business on his own account, i.e. he was incurring the chance of profit or loss. Therefore he was held to be self-employed.

In *Drym Fabricators v. Johnson*, it was held that a member of a workers' co-operative was an employee. The co-operative was registered as a limited company. Consequently it had a legal personality and was capable of employing and dismissing its work force. The complainant was entitled to bring a claim of unfair dismissal against the co-operative.

Whether a company director is an employee is a matter which has been considered by industrial tribunals on several occasions. Where a director is employed at a given salary and granted normal employment rights, it is fairly clear that he is an employee, but where there is no employement contract, difficulties can arise in determining his status. Occasionally clarification of the matter is found in the company's articles of association. In *Parsons v. Albert J. Parsons & Sons Ltd*, the sons of the firm's founder were directors of the company. There were no contracts of service, but the articles provided that the directors should be appointed for life. (Such a provision may be subsequently altered unless the appointment was made before 18 July 1945.) No formal salaries were paid to the directors and they voted themselves a sum described as 'directors' emoluments' at the end of every year. One of the sons was removed from office and applied to an industrial tribunal claiming that he had been unfairly dismissed. It was held that he was not an employee as he was regarded and remunerated as a director.

The loaned employee

If an employee is loaned or hired by one employer to another, it may be necessary to determine which is his current employer, to establish who is liable for any torts (civil wrongs) he may commit or who is responsible for his welfare. If a contract exists between the general and special employer, the contract will have to be examined and interpreted to find the answer. If there is no contract, the arrangements and the degree of control which is exercised over the employee will be the decisive factors.

The general rule is that the permanent general employer will be liable for the negligence of any loaned employee. In *Mersey Docks and Harbour Board v. Coggins and Griffiths*, a firm of stevedores had hired the use of crane with its driver from the Board. The Board stipulated in its contract with the stevedores that 'The drivers so provided shall be the servants of the applicants'. As a consequence of the driver's negligence a checker was injured. The court had to determine whether the general employers of the crane driver or the hirer was liable for the driver's negligence. The hirer could instruct the driver where to go and what to carry, but had no authority to give directions as to the manner in which the crane was to be operated. The Board was held responsible for the driver's negligence, as the driver was appointed by them and they alone had the power to dismiss him.

In *Garrard v. Southey and Co.*, an electrician was loaned to the defendant company. His employers, a firm of electrical contractors, continued to pay him and reserved the right to dismiss him. His day-to-day working was, however, supervised by the defendant company's foreman, a skilled electrician. He was injured when he used a ladder at the defendant's factory which proved to be defective. He sued both employers for negligence. It was held that the temporary employers were liable as they owed him a duty of care to ensure his safety at work.

Although control over an employee may pass to his temporary employers, they do not become his employers. They are only responsible to him and for him as if they were his employers. A contract of employment is a personal contract and cannot be assigned without the consent of the parties (*Nokes v. Doncaster Amalgamated Collieries Ltd*).

In *Denham v. Midland Employers Mutual Assurance Ltd*, a company which had engaged a firm of contractors to undertake work on its premises, provided the services of a labourer. The company continued to pay the labourer although he worked under the control of the contractors. He was killed as a result of the negligence of the contractors' employees and his widow brought an action against the contractors. The contractors claimed an indemnity from one of two insurers, namely Midland Employers Mutual

Assurance, whose policy dealt with liability for accidental injury to 'any person under a contract of service', or Denham, whose policy covered the death of persons other than 'any person under a contract of service'. It was held that Denham must indemnify, for although control had passed to the contractors, they had not become the labourer's employers.

An employee whose contract of employment is varied to permit him to work for a subsidiary company, nevertheless remains an employee of the parent company for the purposes of the EPCA. In *Cross v. Redpath Dorman Long Ltd*, Cross, who was employed by Redpath Dorman Long Ltd (RDL), was sent to work for British Bridge Builders Ltd (BBB), a company partly owned by RDL. As a construction foreman on the Humber bridge his work was under the control of BBB, and variations were made to his contract to include BBB's terms and conditions. He was made redundant and claimed that he had been unfairly dismissed by BBB or alternatively by RDL. It was held that although BBB had use of Cross's services, and in certain circumstances would have been vicariously liable for his actions, he remained an employee of RDL throughout for the purposes of unfair dismissal.

Other employment relationships

There are certain categories of employees who do not fit into the traditional employment pattern. The most important of these are: (*a*) Crown employees (*b*) minors, (*c*) apprentices.

Crown employees

Special provisions apply to Crown employees, for although in practice most civil servants have security of tenure of employment, in theory they may be dismissed at the pleasure of the Crown. Historically the Crown is privileged *vis a vis* contact, and cannot be sued in its own courts. Although the Crown Proceedings Act 1947 and modern employment statutes have made inroads into this doctrine, the Crown is only bound when this is specifically provided for by an Act of Parliament.

Military personnel may not sue the Crown for breach of contract and may not even claim for arrears of pay. Civil servants hold office at the will of the Crown and may be dismissed with or without notice, at the Crown's pleasure. Theory and practice are often different matters however, and civil servants are now regarded as having security of employment.

Civil servants are now also granted the majority of the employment rights afforded to other employees. They may sue for unfair dismissal or sex discrimination, and claim equal pay, but they are not entitled to redundancy payments, minimum periods of notice or written statements of the terms of their employment.

Minors

A minor, i.e. a person under the age of eighteen, is only bound by certain contracts. These are contracts for necessaries and contracts of a beneficial or educational nature. Contracts of employment or apprenticeship which enable him to earn a living are included in the latter category.

In *Doyle v. White City Stadium*, an infant professional boxer held a licence from the British Boxing Board. He was disqualified for delivering a low punch and forfeited his purse. He sued the promoters on the grounds that his contract was not of a beneficial nature. It was held that a penalty clause of this nature, by which the Board sought to improve standards of safety and fairness in professional boxing, was for his benefit.

In *Clements v. LNWR*, an infant porter claimed that his contract of employment was not of a beneficial character as he had foregone his rights under the Employer's Liability Act 1880 to join the company's insurance scheme. It was held that his claim failed, for although the scale of compensation in the company's scheme was lower, it covered more injuries than the statute.

An onerous term may render a minor's contract void. In *Olsen v. Corry & Gravesend Aviation Ltd*, an infant's deed of apprenticeship contained a clause which relieved his employer from all liability for any injury caused to the infant. Such a clause was not deemed to be beneficial and the infant was not bound by it.

Apprentices

A contract of apprenticeship, although a contract of service, is a specialised contract with certain rights and obligations. The essence of the contract is that the master agrees to instruct the apprentice in a trade or calling, and to maintain him. The apprentice agrees to serve the master and learn from him.

The Statute of Artificers 1562 decreed that no person could practise a trade without serving a seven-year term of apprenticeship. This provision was repealed by the Apprentices' Act 1814. Formerly an apprentice was a member of the master's household, but this is rarely found today.

A contract of apprenticeship need not be under seal, i.e. in the form of a deed, but it must be in writing. Although a contract of apprenticeship of a minor is regarded as both necessary and beneficial, it may nevertheless be repudiated by a minor on attaining the age of eighteen or within a reasonable time afterwards. It is therefore usual for a parent or guardian to undertake or guarantee that the minor will complete the apprenticeship.

A number of the terms implied in a contract of apprenticeship are vestiges of the past and are regarded as outmoded in this day and age. An apprentice has a right to lodging to be provided free when he enters the master's household, and must be provided with medicine and medical attendance should this be necessary. The master has the right to chastise an apprentice moderately, but this is now construed as having the right to exercise stricter control over an apprentice than over other employees.

As an apprentice is contractually bound to serve his term of apprenticeship, he may not give notice to terminate the contract. A master's remedy for breach of this obligation is to sue an adult apprentice for breach of contract, or the guarantor for compensation in the case of a minor. A master may not dismiss an apprentice for ordinary misconduct, but he is entitled to do so in cases of serious misconduct, for example where an apprentice was a thief, where an apprentice refused to learn, or where an apprentice was guilty of habitual loose living.

A contract of apprenticeship requires personal performance by both parties and the death of either party will terminate the contract. Termination may also occur on the illness of either party, if the illness is of such a nature or duration as to prevent the performance of the contract. The bankruptcy of the master will also terminate the contract, and if a premium has been paid by the apprentice he may request the trustee in bankruptcy to repay as much as is reasonable, or alternatively to transfer the indentures to another master.

An apprenticeship is also terminated by the death or retirement of a partner in a partnership, unless the apprentice is bound personally to one of the surviving partners rather than to the partnership.

An apprentice is entitled, with minor exceptions, to the benefits of employment protection legislation. An apprentice who is dismissed, other than for serious misconduct, may usually recover damages from his employer. The operation of this legislation is illustrated in the following two cases.

In *Paviour and Thomas v. Whittons Transport*, two apprentices were held to be unfairly dismissed when a receiver gave notice to a number of employees. No arrangements had been made with another employer to take over the contracts of apprenticeship.

In *Townrow v. Phillip Davies*, a solicitor's articled clerk was held not to be unfairly dismissed when ill health forced his employer to amalgamate with another firm of solicitors. The other firm were not prepared to allow a transfer of the articles and the master tried in vain to find alternative articles for the clerk. It was held that the master had acted reasonably in the circumstances.

An apprentice may in these circumstances bring an action for wrongful dismissal. He may claim in respect of loss of earnings and for loss of future prospects, assuming that he had completed his apprenticeship (*Dunk v. Waller*).

Elements of contract

A contract of employment is governed by the general rules of contract. It is an agreement between an employer and an employee which will be enforced by the law. The essential elements of contract must be present, namely:

1 Agreement, i.e. an offer of employment is made by one party and is accepted by the other.
2 Both parties must intend a legally binding relationship to come into existence, with certain obligations imposed on both parties.
3 Consideration (usually remuneration for a service), must be present, unless the contract is made under seal, i.e. by deed.

4 Both parties must have capacity to contract.
5 The reality of the contract must not be affected by mistake.
6 The contract must not be affected by misrepresentation.
7 The contract must not be illegal.

Certain of these elements merit fuller consideration.

1 Agreement comprising offer and acceptance
An offer of employment may be made to one particular individual, to a group of people, or to persons in general. An offer is usually made to a particular individual. It may remain open for a limited time, for example a week or a month, or there may be no time limit stipulated for acceptance. It will remain open until the stipulated time has passed, or a reasonable time has elapsed, or it has been revoked (withdrawn by the person making the offer), or rejected by the other party.

An acceptance must not be qualified (i.e. it must comply with the terms of the offer), and will be effective from the moment of acceptance. In *Taylor v. Furness, Withy & Company Ltd*, a dock worker was allocated by the dock labour board to the defendants. He was given a welcoming letter, an identity card and assigned to work on a ship on his first morning with the defendant company. Later that morning he was informed by the defendant company's manager that he could not be employed as he was not a union member. It was held that he was entitled to be paid his wages from that morning, as a contract of employment was formed when he was handed the letter and the identity card.

2 Intention to create a legal relationship
There must be an intention to create a legal relationship, which excludes a domestic, social arrangement or 'gentleman's agreement'. This contractual requirement has become increasingly important in determining whether a collective agreement is binding on the parties (see page 20).

3 Consideration
The element of consideration is necessary to distinguish a contract from a promise to perform a gratuitous service. The usual form of consideration in a contract of employment consists of an employer's

promise to pay wages in return for an employee's promise to undertake work.

4 Capacity to contract

Most adults are competent to enter into a contract of employment. Certain classes of employees, such as Crown employees, minors and apprentices are subject to special rules (see pages 9–12).

5 Mistake

Only certain categories of mistake affect a contract and render it void. A mistake as to the nature of a document may invalidate a contract, but a mistake as to the contents of a document is inoperative, and the parties will be bound.

6 Misrepresentation

An untrue statement which induces a person to enter into a contract may render a contract voidable at the option of the misled party. An employee is under no obligation to volunteer adverse information, except in certain circumstances (*Sybron Corporation v. Rochem Ltd* – see p. 42). In *Fletcher v. Krell*, a governess who described herself as a spinster, although a divorcee, was held not to have misled her employer. She recovered damages for breach of contract when he refused to employ her.

In *Cork v. Kirby Maclean*, it was held that an employee was not under a duty to disclose to his employer that he was an epileptic.

An employee's dismissal for not disclosing a previous criminal conviction will be unfair if the conviction is 'spent' under the Rehabilitation of Offenders Act 1974. A conviction is 'spent' after varying periods according to the gravity of the sentence. Certain professions, offices and employments are excluded from the provisions of this Act.

7 Illegality

A contract which contravenes the provisions of a statute, or is considered to be contrary to public policy is illegal and will not be enforced. The following are examples of contracts which are *illegal at statute*.

(*a*) The Truck Acts provide that the wages of certain employees (workmen) may only be paid in a certain manner, and that only certain deductions from these wages are permissable. Any other form of payment or any other deduction is illegal (see Chapter 6).

(*b*) Section 140 of the EPCA provides that any agreement which seeks to exclude or limit any provision of the EPCA, or which seeks to preclude a person from complaining to an industrial tribunal or bringing proceedings before it, is void.

(*c*) The preamble to the Sex Discrimination Act 1975 reads: 'An Act to render unlawful certain kinds of sex discrimination and discrimination on the ground of marriage . . .'

Various forms of *illegality* may arise *at common law* in relation to contracts of employment. The most important of these – contracts in restraint of trade – are dealt with in Chapter 5. The following cases are examples of illegality at common law.

(*a*) A contract may contain a servile incident. In *Eastham v. Newcastle United FC*, a footballer sought a declaration that the retain and transfer system used by the Football League was void. Under this system a club was able to place a player on its retained list at the end of his annual contract if he did not agree to the club's new terms. He could only be employed by his club if he accepted those terms and could only be transferred if the fee asked by his club was paid by the other club. The declaration was granted and this led to the abolition of the maximum wage structure, under which professional footballers were paid a pittance for their services.

(*b*) A contract for sexually immoral purposes is an illegal contract and will not be enforced by the courts. If, however, the immorality occurred in the mode of performing an otherwise lawful contract, an employee will not be debarred from enforcing the terms of the contract. In *Coral Leisure Group v. Barnett*, Barnett was employed as a public relations executive by a casino. In the course of his employment, he alleged that he procured and paid for prostitutes for the use of the casino's customers. He was later dismissed and claimed damages for unfair dismissal. The employers claimed that the dismissal was justified, but questioned Barnett's right to enforce an illegal contract. (The company at no time agreed that Barnett had actually procured on their behalf.) The tribunal held that it had the jurisdiction to hear the case as on Barnett's pleadings the immoral purposes were not part of an otherwise lawful contract.

(*c*) A contract of employment involving tax evasion by either the employer or employee is void for illegality in certain cases. The majority of the cases heard by the courts or tribunals under this heading have involved the payment of tax free sums to individual employees. There is nothing necessarily wrong or illegal in agreeing to pay a sum free of income tax, to an employee, as long as the employer pays the tax in respect of that payment to the Revenue (du Parcq LJ in *Miller v. Karlinski*).

If a court or tribunal decides that an employee is aware of the illegal nature of a contract of employment it will declare the whole of the contract to be invalid. The employee will find that he will not be regarded as an employed person and will be unable to claim the various statutory employment benefits, such as redundancy payments and compensation for unfair dismissal.

In *Corby v. Morrison*, an employee was paid, in addition to her normal wage, an extra £5 a week free of income tax and social security liability. Although the employee did not intend to defraud the Inland Revenue, she knew that she was in receipt of tax-free payments. Mrs Corby was later dismissed and brought an action for unfair dismissal. It was held that the contract was unenforceable, and that the tribunal had no jurisdiction to hear the case as she had knowingly been a party to a deception on the Revenue.

If an employee is unaware of the employer's illegal performance of a contract, the employee can enforce the terms of the contract. This is so, even though the employee ought to have appreciated the position, but did not do so. In *Newland v. Simons and Waller (Hairdressers) Ltd*, a hairdresser was paid her wages out of the shop till every Saturday morning. She never received any pay statement, although she received a form P60 at the end of the financial year. Although she should have realised from the form P60 that proper deductions were not being made from her wages, she did not do so. She was dismissed, and it was held that as she was unaware of the illegal nature of the contract, she was entitled to bring an action for unfair dismissal.

2

The Sources of a Contract of Employment

Unlike the majority of commercial contracts, few contracts of employment contain all the written details of the terms of a contract. Many of the essential terms of a contract of employment are to be found in works' rules and collective agreements, or are derived from the custom or practice in a particular industry.

Two forms of contracts of employment are required to be in writing, that of a seaman and a contract of apprenticeship (see page 10). The Merchant Shipping Act 1970 requires an agreement for the engagement of a seaman on a ship registered in the United Kingdom to be signed by both parties. The aim and provisions of the 'crew agreement' must be approved by the Department of Trade and Industry.

Written particulars of the contract of employment

An employer is, however, obliged to supply an employee, within thirteen weeks of the commencement of employment, with a written statement of certain terms of a contract of employment (EPCA section 1). These are:

1   The names of the parties to the contract;
2   The date of commencement of the employment;
3   Whether any employment with a previous employer counts as part of the employee's period of continuous employment, and if so, what period;
4   The scale or rate of remuneration, or the method of calculating remuneration;

5   The intervals at which remuneration is paid, i.e. weekly, monthly, or some other period;

6   Any terms and conditions relating to hours of work (including any relating to normal working hours);

7   Any terms and conditions relating to:

   (*a*)   Entitlement to holidays, including public holidays, and holiday pay (sufficient particulars must be given so as to enable an employee's entitlement to be precisely calculated);

   (*b*)   Incapacity for work due to sickness or injury, including any provision for sick pay;

   (*c*)   Pensions and pension schemes;

8   The length of notice required on either side to terminate the contract;

9   The title of the job which the employee is employed to do;

10   Any disciplinary rules applicable to the employee;

11   The procedure for appeal against any disciplinary action and for seeking redress of any grievance relating to the employment;

12   Whether a contracting-out certificate, relating to the state pension scheme, is in force for that employment.

The statement may refer an employee, for all or any of the particulars, to some document which there is reasonable opportunity of reading in the course of employment, or which is made reasonably accessible in some other way.

An employer is only obliged to furnish this statement to employees in full-time employment, i.e. those who normally work more than sixteen hours per week. Additionally the obligation to provide details of terms 1–9 only applies if these terms exist. If there are no fixed particulars in regard to those items, this fact must be stated.

An employee must be informed, within one month, of any changes in the terms of his employment. He must be informed of the nature of the changes either by means of a written statement or by some other means, for example on a notice board, which must be reasonably accessible.

An employee who leaves an employer, but returns to the same employment within six months need not be given these particulars again. However, if any changes have occurred in the terms of the contract, these must be communicated to him.

These written particulars do not constitute a written contract between the parties, but nevertheless provide very strong evidence of the employer's view of the contractual terms. Only if an employer states clearly that the document constitute the terms of the contract of employment, and the employee signifies his acceptance of the document, as a contractual document, will its terms bind on both parties. In *Systems Floors (UK) Ltd v. Daniel* the employer was able to provide oral evidence to prove that an employee's contract of employment commenced at a later date than that shown in the written particulars.

If an employer fails to provide an employee with those particulars, the employee may apply for relief to an industrial tribunal. The tribunal will then ascertain the particulars and state them accordingly.

Works' rules

Many employers lay down works' or company rules. These may form part of an employee's contract of employment, or they may be regarded as instructions to an employee as to how the work should be done. The distinction is important as any variation of the terms of a contract may only be achieved with the agreement of both parties, while an employer may unilaterally vary and amend any instructions to an employee. However, such instructions must be clear, reasonable and unambiguous.

The rules may also be regarded as an indication of company policy on a particular matter. In *Jeffries v. BP Tanker Co. Ltd*, a ship's officer was held to have been fairly dismissed after he had suffered two heart attacks. The company's rules laid down that an employee with a history of cardiac disease should not be employed at sea. The rule was therefore in the nature of company policy.

A failure by an employee to obey new or amended instructions would be regarded as a breach of a duty to obey lawful orders. In *Secretary of State for Employment v. ASLEF*, members of the railway union threatened a 'work to rule' by their literal interpretation of the rule book, which would undoubtedly have disrupted train services. The Court of Appeal held that this would constitute a breach of contract as the employees would be in breach of an implied term in threatening to impede and disrupt their employer's business.

Collective agreements

A majority of the workers in the UK are members of trade unions which have negotiated collective agreements with employers or groups of employers. Collective agreements are regarded as having two main functions:

1 Regulating the relationship between the parties, i.e. the trade unions and the employer(s). These are usually procedural agreements which outline the procedure to be taken in the event of disagreement, e.g. defining stages of procedure, setting up machinery for negotiation or conciliation, and so on.
2 Regulating the terms and conditions of individual contracts of employment, e.g. pay, hours of work, holidays, overtime.

Collective agreements may also deal with the engagement or non-engagement, termination of employment, or suspension of workers; allocation of work or duties of employment; matters of discipline; membership or non-membership of a trade union; and the right of a trade union to represent workers in these matters (TULRA, section 29).

Section 28 of TULRA provides that a collective agreement made before 1 December 1971, or after 31 July 1974, is conclusively presumed not to have been intended by the parties to be a legally enforceable contract, unless the agreement is in writing and contains a provision that the parties intend it to be legally enforceable. Any collective agreement made between the two previous dates is presumed to be legally enforceable, unless it contains an express exclusion clause stating otherwise. If the collective agreement was not made between the above dates, an employer will be unable to enforce its terms against a trade union and a trade union will be unable to enforce its terms against an employer.

It is generally accepted that in the majority of cases the terms of a collective agreement do not bind an individual employee, who cannot enforce these terms against an employer, and vice versa.

Other reasons for this view (apart from the statutory presumption of section 28 of TULRA) are as follows:

1   As the employee was not a party to the agreement, a contract does not exist between him and the employer, i.e. there is no *privity* of contract;
2   The terms of many collective agreements are vague and therefore incapable of being contractual;
3   The courts are reluctant to imply that a trade union is acting as an agent for its members, i.e. bringing its members into a contractual relationship with an employer;
4   The parties do not intend to be legally bound, i.e. it is regarded as an agreement which is binding in honour only.

In *Ford Motor Co. Ltd v. Amalgamated Union of Engineering and Foundry Workers*, the Ford Company entered into an agreement, by a majority decision, with nineteen unions, relating to procedures, conditions and wages. Some of the minority felt aggrieved by the decision and immediately began an unofficial strike. This was contrary to one of the terms of the agreement which provided that certain procedures would be followed before a stoppage of work occurred. The larger unions, who had supported the majority, then decided to make the strike official. Ford then sought an injunction for breach of the agreement. It was held that the agreement was not a contract and was binding in honour only. It could therefore be broken with impunity by either party.

Although the majority of collective agreements do not bind the parties in law, there are nevertheless statutory provisions which seek to encourage and promote collective bargaining. An employer has a general duty to disclose information to an independent trade union for the purposes of collective bargaining. If he fails or refuses to do so, the trade union concerned may complain to the Central Arbitration Committee (CAC), which may make an award relating to the terms and conditions of service which then form part of the employee's contract of employment. This award is binding on the employer.

The Advisory Conciliation and Arbitration Service (ACAS) has produced a Code of Practice which deals with 'the disclosure of information to trade unions for collective bargaining purposes'. The

Code gives specific examples of information which could be of relevance in certain bargaining situations. These include pay and benefits, conditions of service, manpower structure, performance and productivity, and the financial structure of the undertaking.

The terms of a collective agreement may however bind an employee if they are incorporated into his contract of employment. This incorporation may be either express or implied.

Express incorporation

The contract may contain an express provision that it is to be subject to the terms of a collective agreement.

In *National Coal Board v. Galley*, a written contract provided that Galley's wages and working conditions should be regulated by such national agreements as might be in force for the time being. A national agreement later signed between Galley's union and the NCB provided that 'deputies should work such days or part days in each week as may reasonably be required.' It was held that Galley's refusal to work a Saturday shift amounted to a breach of contract, as the terms of the agreement were incorporated in his contract of service.

In *Camden Exhibition & Display Ltd v. Lynott*, the written particulars of the contract of employment given to an employee provided that his hours of work were to be in accordance with the terms of the national joint council for the exhibition industry. It was held that these terms had become incorporated in his contract of employment.

Implied incorporation

A term may be incorporated by implication into an individual's employment contract if it is regarded as appropriate. Wages, hours of work and holiday entitlement are appropriate, as they relate solely to the individual. Such matters as machinery for settling disputes are not regarded as appropriate, as they do not relate solely to an individual's contract of employment.

In the last century, agreements between master printers and compositors were regulated by committees of each body. In *Hill v. Levey*, it was held that these agreements had become incorporated into every engagement. In *McLea v. Essex Hire Ltd*, a seaman was bound by the terms of an agreement made by the National Maritime Board, the negotiating body for the industry.

The terms of a collective agreement may be regarded as unsuitable for incorporation in a contract. In *Young v. Canadian Northern Railway*, an agreement between the CNR and a trade union of which Young was not a member, that in the event of redundancy, the principle of 'last in first out' should apply, was held not to have been incorporated into Young's contract of employment. His claim for wrongful dismissal, on the basis that the company's redundancy provisions did not accord with the terms of a collective agreement, therefore failed.

Problems are encountered when dealing with the position of non-unionists or individuals who have resigned from a union. In *Singh v. British Steel Corporation*, the plaintiff worked a fifteen day shift system over a five day week. He later resigned from the union. The union later negotiated a new shift system of a twenty-one day shift over seven weeks. He refused to work the new system and was dismissed. It was held that his dismissal was unfair as he was subject to the terms of the original contract. The new terms had not been incorporated into his contract.

Incorporation by statute

Various statutes provide that certain groups of employees are bound by agreements entered into by certain negotiating bodies, or are subject to an award of a particular arbitration body, for example various wages councils seek to protect the interests of non-unionised employees or employees who are not protected by a strong union.

Conflicting collective agreements

In cases where there are conflicting collective agreements governing an employee's contract, the law appears uncertain and obscure. In *Loman and Henderson v. Merseyside Transport Services Ltd*, a national agreement provided for a forty-one hour week, while the local agreement provided for a sixty-eight hour week. An employee who was made redundant claimed that the computation of the average weekly wage should be based on the local agreement. It was held that the local agreement was a gentleman's agreement, which was not intended to have a contractual effect. In *Clift v. West Riding*

County Council, an employee's pay was based on a local agreement, which was not as remunerative as the national agreement. It was held that as the local agreement was later in time, it should prevail.

This principle was not followed in *Gascol Conversions v. Mercer*, where Mercer was employed on a basis of a fifty-four hour week. A national agreement was concluded in 1971, which provided a forty hour week with optional overtime. It also provided that a national agreement should take precedence over a local agreement. A local agreement was concluded in 1971, which provided for a fifty-four hour week. The Court of Appeal decided that the terms of the national agreement prevailed.

Many collective agreements now contain provisions as to which agreement should prevail in the case of such conflict.

No strike clause

Any terms of a collective agreement which prohibit or restrict the rights of a worker to engage in a strike or other industrial action, for example a no strike clause, will not be incorporated into a worker's contract of employment unless the following conditions are met.

The collective agreement must be in writing, and must contain a provision which expressly states that those terms shall or may be incorporated into the worker's contract. It must be reasonably accessible to the employee at his place of work and available for consultation during working hours. The trade union which was party to the collective agreement must be an independent union. The worker's contract must expressly or implicitly incorporate these terms into the contract (TULRA section 18.1).

Custom

On occasions an implied term in an individual contract of employment may be derived from a trade practice or custom in a particular industry or place of employment. Such a custom must be certain, reasonable and notorious, that is, well established.

In *Sagar v. Ridehalgh*, it was held that the practice of deducting sums from a weaver's wages for bad workmanship was an established custom and was a term of each weaver's contract of employment.

In *Bird v. British Celanese* an employee was suspended without pay for two days. It was held that suspension without pay was an established practice of the defendant employer and was an implied term of each employee's contract of employment.

A custom which dates back many centuries is pertinent to the relationship of a domestic servant and an employer. In the absence of other terms, the hiring of a domestic servant may be terminated by a customary month's notice. The close proximity of such a relationship makes it desirable that this type of contract can be terminated without undue delay.

3

Employer's Duties

The duties owed by an employer to an employee depend on the terms of the contract of employment. In the absence of any specific agreement the following duties are implied:

1 To remunerate the employee;
2 In certain circumstances to provide work for the employee;
3 To indemnify the employee;
4 To treat the employee with respect;
5 To permit time off for public duties;
6 To meet safety requirements.

An employer is under no obligation to provide a reference, but should he do so he owes certain obligations to the employee (see page 31).

An employer also owes a duty (in certain circumstances) to a third party to compensate that person for any damage or injury occasioned by the tortious (wrongful) act of an employee. This is known as the doctrine of *vicarious liability* and is dealt with in the final part of the chapter.

1 To remunerate

An employer must pay the employee the agreed remuneration. If this has not been determined in advance, the employer must pay the employee a reasonable sum. The payment of wages is dealt with in Chapter 6.

2 To provide work

As a general rule an employer has no obligation to provide work for an employee, as long as he continues to pay the agreed wages. Asquish J's statement in *Collier v. Sunday Referee Publication Co. Ltd* is often quoted as a simple illustration of the rule: 'Provided I pay my cook her wages regularly, she cannot complain if I choose to take any or all of my meals out'.

There are situations where there is an implied duty to provide work as distinct from merely paying wages, as the following examples show.

(*a*) Where the work provides the employee with an opportunity to enhance his reputation by publicity, for without the work there can be no enhancement. In *Clayton & Waller Ltd v. Oliver*, an actor was promised a leading role in a West End musical. The offer was subsequently withdrawn, and he was offered a lesser role, but at the previously negotiated salary. He refused and was awarded substantial damages for loss of publicity.

(*b*) Where an employee is paid on a piecework or commission basis. In *Turner v. Goldsmith*, a commercial traveller's pay was based on the amount of commission earned. It was held that he must be given a reasonable opportunity to travel and thereby earn his commission.

In *Baumann v. Hulton Press*, a journalist/photographer was paid a retainer of £10 a week and was to be available to undertake commissioned work from the defendants at all reasonable times. It was held that there was an implied term in his contract that the defendants would give him sufficient work to enable him to earn what the parties must have contemplated that he should earn.

In *Devonald v. Rosser*, a piece-worker, given a month's notice by his employers, was entitled to damages when his employers immediately closed down the works where he was employed. It was held that there was an implied term in his contract that his employers would provide him with work during the period of notice.

In *Langston v. Amalgamated Union of Engineering Workers*, an employee was suspended on full pay by his employers in response to a union threat to call a strike if this course of action was not adopted. The employer was held to be in breach of contract as the employee was deprived of the opportunity to earn additional payments for night shift or overtime working.

(c) Where the employee is a skilled worker, and the provision of work is necessary for the maintenance and development of skills. In *Breach v. Epsylon Industries*, a chief engineer was left with no work after his employers gradually transferred their engineering work overseas. It was held that the failure to provide him with work amounted to a repudiation of the contract.

Lord Denning has on several occasions suggested that an employee has a right to be provided with work. In *Langston v. Amalgamated Union of Engineering Workers*, he stated that 'it is arguable that in these days a man has, by reason of an implication in the contract, a right to work'. In *Nagle v. Fielden* some eight years previously, he stated 'a man's right to work at his trade or profession is just as important to him, or perhaps more important than, his rights of property'. He also referred to the *Industrial Relations Code of Practice* which provides in paragraph 9, that 'management should recognise the employee's need to achieve a sense of satisfaction in his job and should provide for it so far as is practicable'.

Where an employer, through no fault of his own, is unable to provide work, he is under no obligation to pay wages. In *Browning v. Crumlin Valley Collieries Ltd*, a mine was closed to enable urgent repairs to be carried out to the mine shafts. It was held that the employees were not entitled to compensation for lost wages during the time of the closure.

3 To indemnify

An employee is entitled to an indemnity if he incurs any expense, loss or liability in carrying out his employer's instructions, if there is an express or implied term to this effect in the contract of employment. The question of indemnity usually arises in situations when an employee is acting, within his authority, as an agent for his employer. In *Re Famatina Development Corporation*, a consulting engineer in compiling a report for a company, reported matters which were allegedly defamatory of the managing director. He was entitled to an indemnity for the costs incurred in subsequently defending a libel action. As he had been engaged to report fully on the company's activities, his duties were much wider than those of an ordinary consulting engineer.

This right of indemnity extends to the commission of an illegal act, as long as the employee is unaware of its illegal nature. In *Burrows v. Rhodes*, an employee, induced by a fraudulent statement to re-enlist in the armed forces of the British South Africa Company, took part in the ill-fated Jameson raid. As he believed the venture to be legal, he was able to recover damages in respect of the injuries he had received.

A more commonplace situation was encountered in *Gregory v. Ford* when an employee injured a third party by his negligent driving. The employee was not aware that the vehicle was not insured. The third party obtained judgment against both the employer and the employee. As the employee was unaware of the illegal nature of the act, he was entitled to an indemnity in respect of the third party's claim.

An employee who is aware of the illegal character of an act may refuse to carry out such an act, and will not be in breach of a duty to obey his employer. If he is aware of the illegality he is not entitled to an indemnity.

4 To treat with respect

An implied duty of mutual respect exists in every employer/ employee relationship. Although this is a vague concept which is often difficult to define, it has nevertheless been re-stated and re-affirmed in recent years. In *Donovan v. Invicta Airways Ltd*, it was stated that each of the parties should treat the other with such a degree of consideration and courtesy as would enable the contract to be fulfilled.

This is clearly shown in the provisions relating to unfair dismissal, and the relevant paragraphs of the Code of Practice dealing with disciplinary practice and procedures in employment. An employer must give adequate training to his employees, keep records and is not entitled, (except in the gravest cases), to dismiss his employees without adequate warnings and an opportunity of improvement.

An employer must not behave in an unreasonable manner and thereby damage or destroy the trust and mutual confidence that should exist in the relationship. An employee may treat the contract of employment as repudiated if an employer's conduct is so grossly unreasonable as to be in effect a constructive dismissal (see page 105).

An employer who wishes to rid himself of an employee or alter the terms of the employment, without becoming liable to pay a redundancy payment or compensation for unfair dismissal, cannot do so by making the employee's life so uncomfortable that he either resigns or accepts revised contractual terms. In this situation an employer would be in breach of the duty of mutual respect. In *Woods v. WM Car Services Ltd*, Lord Denning stated: 'Just as a servant must be good and faithful, so an employer must be good and considerate . . . in modern times an employer can be guilty of misconduct justifying the employee in leaving at once without notice'.

5 To permit time off for public duties

Employers are required under certain circumstances to permit employees who hold certain public positions to have reasonable time off to perform the duties associated with these positions. These provisions apply to employees who are: justices of the peace; members of a local authority; members of any statutory tribunal; members of a Regional or District Health Authority; members of the managing or governing body of an educational establishment maintained by a local education authority; or members of a water authority.

An employee is entitled to reasonable time off for any duties incurred by membership of any of these bodies. A definition of 'reasonable time off' depends on the circumstances, but the following factors should be taken into consideration:

1 How much time off is required in general to perform these duties, and how much time off is required on the particular occasion in question;
2 How much time off has already been permitted for this purpose or for trade union duties and/or activities;
3 The circumstances of the employer's business and the effect of the employee's absence upon it.

An employer is under no obligation to pay an employee for any time taken off in connection with public duties, unless an agreement to do so has been entered into with the employer or the trade union.

6 To meet safety requirements

An employer owes a duty at common law and statute to take reasonable care for the safety of his employees. This is dealt with in detail in Chapter 5.

Provision of a reference

An employer is not obliged to provide an employee or former employee with a reference or testimonial, or to answer questions from a third party relating to an employee's character.

A testimonial is usually given to an employee and becomes his personal property, while a reference is usually communicated in confidence to a prospective employer. An employer who provides a reference or testimonial may in certain circumstances incur liability on the document to the employee (or former employee) or to a third party.

An employee may allege that a statement contained in the document was defamatory, i.e. was a false statement which lowered his reputation in the eyes of right thinking members of society. The employer may plead that the statement was substantially true, but is more likely to rely on the defence of *qualified privilege*. This protects an employer who makes a statement in the performance of a legal or moral duty to a person who has a corresponding interest or duty in receiving it, e.g. a prospective employer. The statement must be made honestly, with a belief in its truth, and must be free from malice.

An employer who recommends an employee to a third party in terms which he knows to be false may incur liability if the third party suffers damage as a result of his recommendation. In *Technovision v. Reed*, the plaintiff hired an accountant, relying on an outstanding reference given by his previous employer, the defendant. The employee stole from Technovision, and it emerged that he had previously stolen from Reed, who admitted that he had put his signature to a blank piece of headed notepaper. Technovision successfully sued Reed for damages.

An employer may also incur liability if a third party suffers financial injury as a result of a statement made carelessly or negligently by him (*Hedley Byrne & Co. Ltd v. Heller & Partners Ltd*).

An employer who is asked for a reference in respect of an employee whose previous conviction is spent, is under an obligation not to refer to any spent conviction or to any circumstances ancillary to it (The Rehabilitation of Offenders Act 1974). It also provides that he shall not incur any liability to a third party for not disclosing a spent conviction.

Vicarious liability

An employer is liable for any tort (civil wrong), committed by an employee in the course of employment, if it causes damage to another party. This is known as vicarious liability.

As an employee's wrongful act must arise in the course of his employment, an employer is clearly liable for a tort which he has expressly authorised to be committed. He is also liable for any act or omission which results in the commission of a tort. In *Gregory v. Piper*, an employee who was laying rubble near a neighbour's wall was expressly instructed by his employer not to allow the rubble to come into contact with the wall. Unfortunately the instructions were not carried out and the employer was liable to his neighbour in trespass.

An employer is also liable if an employee 'does fraudulently that which he was authorised to do honestly or if he does mistakenly that which he was authorised to do correctly'. (Salmon on Torts, 18th ed.). The following cases illustrate this principle.

In *Bayley v. Manchester, Sheffield and Lincolnshire Railway Company*, a railway porter removed a passenger from a train by force, stating 'You are in the wrong train, you must come out'. The Railway Company was held liable for the injury caused to that passenger.

In *Jefferson v. Derbyshire Farmers*, a youth employed by Derbyshire Farmers lit a cigarette when filling a tin with inflammable spirit. The resulting explosion and fire burned down the garage. The employer was held liable for the damage as the youth was acting within the scope of his employment.

An employer cannot avoid liability by showing that he had expressly forbidden an employee to use the particular mode of work. In *Limpus v. London General Omnibus Company Ltd*, the company had expressly forbidden its bus drivers 'to race with or obstruct another omnibus, or hinder or annoy the driver or conductor thereof'. A driver nevertheless obstructed one of Limpus' horse-drawn buses and caused damage to the bus and the horses. It was held that the bus company was liable for the acts of its employees.

An employer may be vicariously liable if an employee takes steps to protect the employer's property in an emergency. The employee's actions are often excessive but in the majority of cases the courts have decided that the employer is liable, for it is his interests that are being protected. In *Poland v. John Parr and Sons*, an employee mistakenly believed that a boy was about to steal a bag of sugar from his employer's wagon. He struck the boy, who fell under the wagon and had his leg amputated as a result of his injuries. It was held that the employer was liable.

If the act in question is dictated by the personal considerations of the employee, rather than the employer's interests, it may well be outside the scope of the employment. In *Daniels v. Whetstone Entertainments*, a dance hall bouncer, not content with evicting a reveller from the club, carried on assaulting him outside the club. He subsequently died from those injuries. It was held that the continuation of the assault took it outside the scope of the employer's liability.

An employer may be liable if an employee who is authorised to drive a vehicle permits an unauthorised person to drive in his place. This may well constitute a wrongful method of fulfilling an authorised act. In *Ilkiw v. Samuels*, a lorry driver allowed a third party to move a lorry to make room for other lorries, who were waiting to load. The lorry driver, who was at the back of the lorry covering the load, was unaware that the third party was incompetent. The third party crashed the lorry into a conveyor belt and injured the plaintiff. The lorry driver's employers were held liable for the damages resulting from the accident, as the driver was held to be in charge of the vehicle, although he was not at the controls at the time of the accident.

An employer will not generally be liable where, despite orders to the contrary, an employee gives a lift to a third party. In *Twine v. Bean's Express* it was held that the employee's act in giving a lift was outside the scope of his employment. In *Conway v. George Wimpey* it was held that the third party was a trespasser.

The courts have distinguished between a gratuitous lift, and the situation where an employee, despite orders to the contrary, carries a passenger in furtherance of a purpose which is related to the employer's business. In *Rose v. Plenty*, a milkman used the services of a thirteen-year-old boy, despite instructions to the contrary. He also paid him a weekly sum for his services. The boy was injured as a result of the employee's negligence. It was held that the employer was liable, as the boy's services were used in furtherance of the employer's business.

An employer will not be liable if the employee's act was outside the scope of the employment, i.e. the employee was engaged on an activity for which he was not employed. In *Beard v. London General Omnibus Company*, a bus conductor, in the driver's absence, drove a bus and injured the plaintiff. The bus company were not liable as the bus conductor's actions were outside the scope of his duties.

For an employer to be liable to a third party, the employee must have been using the employer's property on his employer's business. If an employee injures a third party while using his employer's property in circumstances where there is no connection with the employer's business, the employer bears no liability. In *Rayner v. Mitchell*, a drayman, without permission, took a van out of his employer's stables to deliver a coffin to a relative's house. On the return journey he collected some empty beer barrels and was later involved in an accident. It was held that the employer was not liable as the act of collecting the barrels did not convert an unauthorised journey into an authorised journey.

An employer may not be vicariously liable where an employee deviates from his work or an authorised route to undertake some business of his own. Judges in the last century described an employee's actions in this situation as 'a frolic of his own'. In general, a slight deviation from an authorised route does not detract from the main purpose of the journey which is the delivery of the employer's goods. In these circumstances the employer will be liable for any torts committed in the course of his journey.

An employee's criminal conduct may be regarded as being in the course of his employment if a third party suffers as a result of the employee's criminal act. In *Morris v. C. W. Martin & Sons*, an employee's theft of a mink stole, sent for cleaning to his employers, resulted in his employers being found liable to recompense the plaintiff as the employee had been entrusted with the article in the course of his employment.

An employer who is sued by a third party, following an employee's negligent act, has the right to claim an indemnity from the employee in question, i.e. an employer may recover from the employee the amount paid as damages to the third party (*Lister v. Romford Ice and Cold Storage Co. Ltd* – see page 38).

Where an employer has been negligent and partially contributed to the negligent act, he may not recover the whole amount from the employee, only that proportion that is attributable to the employee's negligence, i.e. a contribution from the employee (*Jones v. Manchester Corporation* – see page 39).

Liability for the torts of an independent contractor

An employer who uses the services of an independent contractor is generally not liable for any torts committed by the independent contractor. In the following circumstances liability will be imposed:

1 Where the employer authorises the commission of a tort, for example instructing the contractor to tip waste on another person's land (the tort of trespass).

2 Where the employer instructs an independent contractor to undertake work which is inherently dangerous. In *Honeywill-Stein v. Larkin Brothers Ltd*, an employer was held liable for the contractor's negligence when magnesium flares used for taking indoor photographs set light to theatre curtains and caused substantial damage.

3 Where work is being done by the contractor on or in a highway. An employer in these cases usually has a statutory duty to undertake work which would otherwise be classed as a nuisance, but is

nevertheless liable for injuries caused by the negligence of an independent contractor. In *Holliday v. National Telephone Company*, a plumber engaged by the Telephone Company negligently used a blowlamp which exploded and injured a passer-by. The company was liable for the contractor's negligence.

4   If a nuisance is created as a result of a contractor's work on the employer's land, the employer will be liable to those parties whose use of their land is affected by the nuisance. Examples of such nuisances are smoke, noise, fumes, dust or vibration.

5   Where an absolute duty is imposed by statute on an employer, he cannot evade liability by delegating its performance to a contractor. In *Groves v. Wimbourne*, it was held that a factory owner, under a duty to fence machinery, was liable for the faulty workmanship of the contractor who had erected the fencing on the employer's behalf.

Where an employer is held liable to a third party for the torts of an independent contractor, he will generally be able to claim an indemnity from the contractor.

4

Employee's Duties

The relationship of employer and employee imposes obligations on both parties. Provisions as to remuneration, the hours of work and the main terms of the contract of employment are clearly spelt out in details given to the employee in the Employment Protection (Consolidation) Act. There are however certain rights and obligations which are not provided for by statute, but are nevertheless implied in a contract of employment. These are:

1 To render personal service;
2 To render careful service;
3 To obey reasonable orders;
4 To act in good faith;
5 To serve the employer loyally;
6 To share the benefit of an invention;
7 Not to disclose confidential information.

1 To render personal service

An employee undertakes to render personal service, i.e. to perform in person the contract of employment. He also warrants that he has the necessary skills to perform the work. In *Alidair v. Taylor*, an airline pilot was fairly dismissed as the result of an unsatisfactory landing which endangered the lives of his passengers. The Air Navigation Order provides that 'The operator of an aircraft registered in the UK shall not permit any person to be a member of the crew thereof during any flight . . . unless the operator has satisfied himself that such a person is competent to perform his duties'.

In *Bevan Harris Ltd v. Gair*, a foreman was fairly dismissed after eleven years service (after four warnings) for failing to carry out his tasks in a satisfactory manner.

A court may not compel an employee to fulfill his or her obligations under (*a*) an order for specific performance (or specific implement) of a contract of employment, or (*b*) an injunction (or interdict) restraining a breach or threatened breach of such a contract.

Although an employer cannot compel an employee to work for him, he can nevertheless prevent that employee from working for a rival company, when the employee has entered into a covenant not to work for another employer in that area of work. In 1936 the actress Bette Davis entered into a contract with Warner Bros for one year, renewable for further yearly periods at the option of Warner Bros. She agreed that she would only work as a film artist for Warner Bros. In breach of this agreement she entered into a contract with a rival film company. It was held that Warner Bros were entitled to an injunction to prevent her from working as an actress with a rival company (*Warner Bros v. Nelson*).

An employee cannot compel an employer to continue to employ him. In *Chappell v. The Times Newspapers Ltd*, the National Graphical Association were engaged in a trade dispute with Times Newspapers. The newspapers gave notice that unless the union called off its action its members would be regarded as having terminated their contracts of employment. The employees sought to prevent the newspaper proprietors from taking such action, but were not entitled to such an order.

2   To render careful service

An employee is under an obligation to render careful service to his employer and must exercise skill and care in the course of his employment. The degree of skill and care will obviously depend upon the nature of the contract and the representations made by the employee, i.e. that he has the degree of skill which he professes to have. In *Lister v. Romford Ice Cold Storage Company*, a lorry driver, whilst reversing, injured his 'mate', who subsequently sued the employer for injuries caused by an employee of the firm, i.e. the lorry driver. The driver's 'mate' was in fact the driver's father. He recovered substantial damages for his injuries. The Insurance Company paid the damages and then sued the driver, in the Company's name, to recover the damages paid. It was held that the driver owed the company a duty to perform his work with care and skill and was liable, as he was in breach of this duty.

This principle was recently re-affirmed in *Janata Bank v. Ahmed*, where the assistant general manager of the Bank's London branch was successfully sued for negligence, in that he gave loans to individuals without satisfactory collateral or references: The loans were not repaid and he was held liable in damages.

In *Jones v. Manchester Corporation*, a surgeon's negligence caused the death of a patient. The hospital was held liable for the surgeon's negligence, but was entitled to recover part of the damages from its employee, the surgeon.

3   To obey reasonable orders

An employee must obey reasonable orders given to him by his employer. What is a reasonable order has on several occasions been discussed by the courts. In the last century a representative of a woollen company was ordered by his employer to card wool. He refused to do so and was dismissed. It was held that he was entitled to refuse to do such a menial task and was awarded damages (*Price v. Mouat*).

In *Pepper v. Webb*, a gardener refused, one Saturday morning, to work beyond his normal hours in order to plant flowers for his employer's wife. As he left he added insult to injury by stating 'I couldn't care less about your bloody greenhouse and your sodding garden'. As this was not an isolated incident he was held to have been fairly dismissed.

If an order exposes an employee to the dangers of violence or disease he may rightly refuse to obey such an order. In *Ottoman Bank v. Chakarian*, an Armenian employee was sent to its head office at Constantinople. As he had previously been sentenced to death by the Turkish authorities and had escaped, he asked his employers to transfer him to a branch outside Turkey as he feared for his life. His request was refused. He fled from Constantinople and was dismissed without notice. He successfully brought an action for wrongful dismissal.

However, it must be shown that a danger exists for a claim to be successful. In *Walmseley v. Udec Refrigeration*, an employee was dismissed for refusing to work in Wexford, as he considered that area to be a hot-bed of IRA activity. As he could not substantiate his claim his dismissal was upheld by the court.

An employee may well be in breach of contract if he refuses to work overtime in those cases where there is an implied or tacit agreement that overtime will be worked. Colliery deputies had agreed to work 'such days as may reasonably be required by the management'. Six deputies refused to work on Saturday mornings and were each sued for £3.50 by the National Coal Board for loss of production. It was held that the NCB was entitled to recover this sum from each deputy *(NCB v. Galley* (see p. 22)).

The Court of Appeal has given guidance as to when it may be regarded as reasonable to refuse to obey a lawful order *(Union of Construction Allied Trades and Technicians v. Brain)*. The nature of the order, the circumstances surrounding the giving of that order and the employee's reason for not carrying out the order must all be considered.

Brain, the editor of the union's journal, was sued after the publication of a defematory article relating to an employer in the federation journal. His employers instructed him to settle the libel action but, on the advice of the union's legal officer, he declined to do so. He felt that the undertaking contained in the proposed settlement, that neither he nor the employees or printers should print any further libel relating to the employers' federation, would make him liable for the acts of other parties over whom he had no control. It was held that his subsequent dismissal for refusing to obey a lawful order was unfair, as in the circumstances his refusal was not unreasonable.

The Employment Appeal Tribunal also considered the question of a lawful order in *Davidson v. Maillou Comparisons Ltd*. Employees refused to accept a transfer to different premises when the employers learned that the employees proposed to open a shop in competition a hundred yards from their existing workplace. It was held that they were fairly dismissed as an employer is entitled to take reasonable steps to protect himself against unfair competition.

4 To act in good faith

An employee must show good faith towards his employer. This encompasses a variety of situations. In *Sinclair v. Neighbour*, a manager of a betting shop borrowed £15 from the till to place a bet on horses and deposited an IOU for the money in the till. The following day he retrieved the IOU and repaid the £15. It was held that the employee, though not dishonest, had acted in a manner which was incompatible with his employment as a manager.

An employee must not make a secret profit from his employment. The employer will in these circumstances he entitled to recover the value of the secret profit from the employee. In *Boston Deep Sea Fishing Company v. Ansell*, the company's managing director entered into contracts for constructing fishing smacks and was secretly paid a commission on the contract by the shipbuilders. He also owned shares in an ice-making company which paid, in addition to dividends, a bonus to shareholders who were owners of fishing smacks and who purchased ice from the ice company for use in their ships. These sums were subsequently recovered from Ansell by the plaintiff company.

An employee may not take advantage of his employment to make a profit, which, although not arising in the course of his employment, arises due to his employment. In *Reading v. Attorney General*, Sergeant Reading, who was stationed in Egypt, made a substantial profit by shepherding convoys of lorries carrying illicit spirit through patrol blocks. This money was confiscated by the military authorities. He later unsuccessfully sued the Crown for its return.

An employee who misuses information received in the course of his employment, or who uses that information for his personal benefit, is liable to account to his employer (or former employer) for any profit made in these circumstances. In *Industrial Development Consultants v. Cooley*, Industrial Development Consultants Ltd provided construction consultancy services for gas boards. Its managing director was an architect named Cooley. The Eastern Gas Board offered tenders for building, and Cooley was informed that it was unlikely that IDC Ltd would be given the contract. He realised that he had an excellent opportunity of obtaining the contract for himself and represented to IDC Ltd that he was ill. IDC released him from his contract and he then obtained the benefit of the contract for himself. IDC successfully sued him for the profit he made on the building contracts.

An employee has a duty to report the misconduct of his fellow employees. In *Sybron Corporation v. Rochem Ltd*, a company recovered a pension payment of £13 208 from a senior executive who had been engaged with his subordinates in a conspiracy to set up in direct competition with the company. As a senior executive, his duty was to report the fraudulent activities of his subordinates.

If an employee accepts a bribe or reward from a third party, there is an irrebuttable presumption that he has been influenced in his dealings by that payment. In *Shipway v. Broadwood*, a sale of horses was conditional on their being passed as sound by a veterinary surgeon. The sale was concluded, but the horses were found to be unsound. As the veterinary surgeon had received a commission from the seller, the sale was put aside. The Court of Appeal ruled that it was immaterial whether the commission had any effect on the judgement of the veterinary surgeon.

An employer may not only rescind the contract but also recover the amount of the bribe from the employee. Additionally the Prevention of Corruption Act 1906 provides that the giving and receiving of bribes is a criminal offence.

5 To serve the employer loyally

There is an implied term that an employee shall serve his employer loyally in his business. If an employee harms his employer by any work undertaken in his spare time, there is therefore a breach of this term. In *Hivac v. Park Royal Scientific Investments Company Ltd*, the employees of a firm which manufactured miniature valves worked at weekends and evenings for a competitor, who was also engaged in the manufacture of valves. It was held that an injunction would be granted to prevent this moonlighting.

This does not prevent an employee from working for a competitor. An employee can usefully and profitably employ himself in his free time, in some other capacity, for some other employer. In *Nova Plastics v. Froggatt*, an odd-job man, who worked for a rival company in his spare time, was held to have been unfairly dismissed. Working for a rival employer is not a breach of an implied term of loyal service, unless it can be shown that the employer has suffered harm by the employee's actions.

Restraint of trade

An employer is entitled to incorporate a restraint clause in an employee's contract of service. Such a clause may prevent an employee on leaving his present employment from entering into a similar type of business, either on his own account or with another employer, in a particular area for a certain length of time.

As a restraint clause is *prima facie* void, it is for the employer to justify the restraint on the basis that the restrictions placed on the employee are reasonable in terms of the time, the area of the restraint and the interest to be protected.

Confidential information An employee may use his own skill and knowledge in competition, but he may not use confidential information which could harm his employer's interests (see p. 45).

In *Forster v. Suggett*, an engineer who worked with a glass manufacturing company, and was conversant with secret manufacturing processes, agreed that he would not be engaged in the manufacture of glass products for five years. This covenant was upheld by the courts.

Business and customer connections An employer is entitled to impose a covenant which protects his business connections and prevents his customers from being enticed away by his former employee. A court will only uphold such a covenant if the former employee had personal contact with the employer's customers. In *Fitch v. Dewes*, a solicitor's clerk agreed that he would not on leaving his employment set up in business as a solicitor within seven miles of Tamworth Town Hall. As the clerk had an extensive acquaintance with his employer's clients, this was held to be valid.

In *André v. Bashford*, an apprentice hairdresser agreed that she would not set up in competition within three-quarters of a mile of her former employer's place of business, for six months after leaving his employment. This was also upheld by the court. It is interesting to compare these two cases with *Strange Ltd v. Mann,*, where the manager of a bookmaker's shop covenanted that on leaving his employment he would not be engaged in a similar business within a twelve-mile radius of his present employment. As most of the betting was done over the phone, the defendant had little personal contact with customers. It was held that the covenant was an attempt to stifle competition.

In *Home Counties Dairies Ltd v. Skilton*, a milk roundsman agreed that he would not, within one year after leaving his present employment, sell milk or dairy products to any person who, during the last six months of his employment, had been a customer of the dairy and whom he had served as the dairy's employee. Within days of leaving his employment he started to operate a milk round covering the same area for a competitor. The court granted an injunction to prevent the breach of the restraint. The clause was reasonable and protected a legitimate interest.

In *Spafax Ltd v. Taylor*, a salesman covenanted that he would not, for two years after leaving Spafax's employment, solicit or seek to obtain orders for goods which he dealt with on behalf of Spafax, or any similar goods from anyone to whom he sold goods on Spafax's behalf during the six months prior to his leaving the employment. It was held that the convenant was reasonable.

Area of restraint   Another case illustrates the limitations which the courts will place on the enforcement of a restrictive covenant. In *Marley Tile Co. Ltd v. Johnson*, the defendant agreed that for twelve months after leaving his employment he would not canvass, solicit or deal with Marley's products, or any similar products within any area in which he had been employed during the preceding twelve months. It was held that although the period of twelve months was reasonable, the restriction as to area (covering practically the whole of Devon and Cornwall) was too wide. The covenant was therefore invalid.

The courts have recently adopted a more liberal approach to the interpretation of restraint clauses. In *Littlewoods Organisation v. Harris*, the defendant worked in a senior position for the firm and had access to confidential information as to the organisation and operation of their mail order business. He covenanted that, on leaving his employment, he would not work for their chief rivals, Great Universal Stores (GUS) for a period of twelve months. He resigned to take up a post with GUS. The restraint was world-wide and covered companies associated with GUS which were not in the mail order business. In former times such a restraint would be regarded as void, but the Court of Appeal was prepared to modify the restriction and apply it to the mail order business carried on by GUS in the UK.

6 To share the benefit of an invention

The benefit of an invention made by an employee while in his employer's service belongs to his employer if:

(*a*) It was made by the employee during his normal duties; or
(*b*) It was made outside the course of normal duties, but it was the result of a specific assignment and the circumstances were such that an invention might reasonably be expected to result from those duties; or
(*c*) Because of the employee's particular responsibilities he has a special obligation to further the interests of the employer's undertaking. (section 39, Patents Act 1977).

In all other circumstances an employee's invention belongs to him, and any purported agreement to the contrary is invalid. An employee may, if he so wishes, assign or transfer the benefit of a patent to his employer, usually for a cash payment or a percentage of the profits made by marketing the invention.

In certain circumstances an employee may benefit from his invention, even though the patent belongs to his employer. An employee may apply to the court or to the Comptroller General of Patents for compensation, in the following cases:

(*a*) If the invention proves to be of outstanding benefit to the employer's business; or
(*b*) If the patent had originally been granted to the employee, (who had assigned it to the employer), but the benefit derived by the employee from the assignment is inadequate in relation to that derived by the employer.

An employee must receive by way of compensation 'a fair share (having regard to all the circumstances) of the benefit which the employer has derived from the patent . . .' (section 40, Patents Act 1977).

7 Not to disclose confidential information

An employee is under a duty not to disclose confidential information or material relating to his employer's business. In *Thomas Marshall (Exports) Ltd v. Guinle*, it was stated that there are four elements which may assist the court in identifying confidential information or trade secrets which will be protected. These are:

(a) The owner must believe that the release of the information would be injurous to him or advantageous to his rivals;
(b) The owner must believe that the information is confidential or secret;
(c) These beliefs must be reasonable;
(d) The information must be judged in the light of the usage and practices of the particular trade or industry concerned.

An employer may seek an injunction if he considers that the publication of confidential information or material would be harmful to his business. It must be shown that:

(a) The material to be published is and remains confidential to the employer;
(b) It was given to someone in circumstances which would give rise to a duty of confidence to the employer;
(c) It was passed on, by that person, in breach of confidence.

A document remains of a confidential nature, despite a widespread distribution to a work force, merely by having the word 'Confidential' stamped on it. *(Sun Printers Ltd v. Westminister Press Ltd)*.

An employee is not bound by this duty of confidentiality if he discloses confidential information acquired in his employment which relates to 'misconduct of such a nature that it ought in the public interest to be disclosed to others'. The person to whom such information is disclosed must have a proper interest in receiving it. In *Initial Services Ltd v. Putterill*, it was held that a sales manager was entitled to disclose an arrangement by which his former employers maintained prices, which allegedly contravened the Restrictive Trade Practices Act 1956.

Safety of Employees

An employer is under a duty at common law and under the provisions of the Health and Safety at Work Act 1974 to take reasonable care for the safety of his employees. Section 2.1 of the Health and Safety at Work Act (HSWA) provides that: 'It shall be the duty of every employer to ensure, so far as is reasonably practicable, the health, safety and welfare at work of all his employees'. Section 2.2 states '. . . the matters to which that duty extends include in particular the provision and maintenance of plant and systems of work that are, so far as is reasonably practicable, safe and without risks to health'.

Employer's obligations at common law

In some respects, sections 2.1 and 2.2 of the HSWA restate the general duty which the common law imposes on an employer with regard to the safety of his employees.

An employer does not guarantee that injury will not befall an employee. He merely undertakes that he will take reasonable care, i.e. 'the care which an ordinary prudent employer would take in all the circumstances', and will only be liable if some lack of care on his part fails to prevent an injury to an employee that was reasonably foreseeable. In *Vinney v. Star Paper Mills*, an employee who was instructed to clean a floor on which viscous liquid had been spilt, slipped on the floor whilst cleaning it. It was held that there was no foreseeable risk in such a straightforward task. Another employer was held not to blame where a worker was injured in the general rush to reach the canteen (*Lazarus v. Firestone Tyre Rubber Company*).

An employer's duty in respect of his employee's safety was summarised by Swanwick J. in *Stokes v. Guest Keen and Nettlefold Ltd*:

(a)   An employer must take steps to ensure his employee's safety in the light of knowledge which he has or ought to have;

(b)   An employer is entitled to follow a recognised practice, unless this is clearly unsound;

(c)   He must keep reasonably abreast of developing knowledge and not be too slow in applying it;

(d)   If he has greater than average knowledge of the risk he must take more than average precautions;

(e)   He should weigh up the risks in terms of the likelihood of the occurrence of an injury and the potential consequences, and balance that against the effectiveness, expense and inconvenience of the precautions.

This shows that an employer is only liable if he fails to take positive steps to ensure his employee's safety in the light of current recognised practice and knowledge. When there is a developing area of knowledge, he must keep reasonably abreast of it, and must apply it in a reasonably practical manner.

In *Wright v. Dunlop Rubber Co. & ICI*, the employers had, since 1940, used a substance called Nonox S in the manufacture of tyres. The manufacturers, ICI, later discovered that the product carried the risk of cancer and informed Dunlop of the fact, advising them to screen and test all employees who had been exposed to the product. As this was not done for some considerable time, both Dunlop and ICI were liable to the plaintiff.

An employer is entitled to weigh up the risk in terms of the likelihood of injury, and balance that against the effectiveness of the precautions needed to meet the risk, and the economic consequences of taking or not taking the risk. In *Latimer v. AEC*, a company spread sawdust on the factory floor after a storm had flooded the works. The flood had left a film of oil on the floor and some areas were left untreated due to a shortage of sawdust. It was held that it would be unrealistic to close the factory with consequent loss of wages and production until absolutely safe conditions existed. Latimer was therefore unable to claim damages as a result of slipping on the floor, as the company had, in the circumstances, taken reasonable precautions.

The duty is not collective, but is owed to each employee individually. In *Paris v. Stepney Borough Council*, it was held that an employer owes a greater duty of care to an employee suffering from a physical defect than to other employees. The plaintiff, who was blind in one eye, suffered injury to his good eye whilst working as a fitter, and claimed that he should have been supplied with goggles. It was held that the employer should have taken additional precautions in these circumstances and he was entitled to damages.

An employer's duty is personal and he cannot avoid liability for injury to an employee by delegating his duties, or by obtaining the services of an independent contractor. This is so even if the employer is compelled by statute, or by lack of the requisite knowledge to delegate to a subordinate. In *Wilson & Clyde Coal Co. v. English*, the owner of a mine delegated the task of installing a system of work to an agent. The system proved to be defective and as a result an employee was injured. The owner was held liable, despite the fact that he was bound under the provisions of the Coal Mines Act to delegate this task.

An employer's duty is to provide for the safety of his employee and does not extend to safeguarding the employee's property. A hospital authority was not liable for the loss incurred by a Registrar, whose clothing was stolen from a hostel owned by the authority. Neither was a theatre management liable when a Widow Twankey's costume was stolen from an actor's dressing room (*Deyong v. Shanburn*).

An employer's duty to provide for his employees' safety may be considered under four headings:

1 The provision of a safe system of work.
2 The provision of safe premises.
3 The provision of safe plant and equipment.
4 The provision of competent fellow employees.

1 Safe system of work

What constitutes a safe system can only be determined in the particular circumstances of the case, and will vary according to the nature of the work involved and the general practice in the particular industry. In many kinds of operations there is no uniformity or regularity in the tasks which are encountered. The actual situation at a given time must then be examined to determine whether a safe system is in operation.

The following factors are relevant in deciding whether a reasonably safe system has been established: the physical lay-out of the job; the sequence in which the work is to be carried out; the provision of warnings and notices; the issue of special instructions; and general working conditions.

Where a potentially dangerous task is constantly repeated, an employer is under a duty to devise a safe system which will, as far as is reasonably possible, eliminate the danger. If the task is unusual or complicated the employer should organise and supervise the task. In *Rees v. Cambrian Wagon Works Ltd*, a cog wheel weighing 15 cwt, and measuring 125 cm in diameter and 20 cm in width was being removed from a machine, with the aid of a plank and sloping wedge. As the wedge was not wide enough to keep the plank in position, the plank rocked, and the wheel overbalanced and fatally injured an employee. The employer was held liable as he had not devised a safe system of working for that particular task.

An employer must not only devise a safe system of working, but also ensure that the system is enforced. Nevertheless he is not liable for an injury to an employee if that employee, without the employer's consent or knowledge, departs from the system. In *Woods v. Durable Suites*, the defendant company used synthetic glue in their works with the consequent risk of the employees contracting dermatitis. The employers provided adequate washing facilities and cream, and made widely known to the employees the risk involved if proper precautions were not observed. Unknown to them an employee had disregarded these precautions and contracted dermatitis. The employer was not liable as 'there is no duty at common law, to stand over workmen of age and experience'. In situations where there is an obvious danger the courts have adopted the attitude that an employee cannot be treated like an 'imbecile child'.

An employee who is indifferent to his own safety and who is subsequently injured may find the courts unsympathetic if his employer has provided equipment which would lessen the danger, for example in *Qualcast v. Haynes*, an employee was injured when molten metal spilt on to his feet, from a ladle he was handling. Notices specified that protective boots were available in the stores. As he was not wearing protective boots the employer was held not to be liable.

In *James v. Hepworth and Grandage*, an employee was injured while working in a foundry. The employer displayed notices advising the employees to wear spats. As the employee had not done so, the employer was held not to be liable, despite the fact that the employee could not read. He had seen and understood the use of spats and made a decision not to use them.

A similar conclusion was reached in *McWilliams v. Arrol*, when a steel erector, working without a safety belt, was killed when he fell some hundred feet to the ground. The employer was not liable for although a safety belt was not available on the site, the evidence showed that had it been available it would not have been worn by the employee.

If a danger exists which is not obvious to the employees, the employer is under a duty not only to warn of the danger, but also to convince employees of the necessity of taking precautions. In *Crookall v. Vickers Armstrong* a foundry's sandy floor created a risk of silicosis. Although the employers provided exhaust appliances, they did not sufficiently emphasise to the work force the need to wear masks to overcome the danger of silicosis. The employers were consequently liable for the plaintiff contracting silicosis.

2 Safe premises

An employer must take reasonable care to ensure that the place of work is safe and that steps are taken to minimise any dangers of which he is aware or which are apparent. In *Bath v. BTC*, an employee working on a narrow ledge on a dry dock, fell and was killed. As the possibility of injury was apparent, the employer was held liable for not providing adequate safety measures, e.g. a safety net.

The employer must also provide safe access to and from the place of work. In *Bryden v. Stewart*, it was held that the owner of a coal mine had not provided a safe access to and from the pit when a stone from the side of the mine shaft fell into an open cage and killed one of the miners.

An employer remains liable for the safety of his employees, even though an employee is working in premises occupied by a third party. However, he cannot be held responsible for the state of premises which are not under his control. In *Cilia v. H. M. James & Sons*, a plumber's mate was electrocuted when installing new plumbing in a building. The employer was not liable as the building was not occupied by him, and he was unaware of the defective electric circuit in the building.

Although the structure of the premises is outside the employer's control, he remains under a duty to exercise reasonable care to safeguard the employee against dangers which he should anticipate and which can be averted. He must provide proper safety equipment and give instructions, if this appears necessary.

In *General Cleaning Contractors Ltd v. Christmas*, a window cleaner, cleaning the outside of the windows of the Caledonian Club, fell when a window sash fell on his hand. Although it was not possible to fit safety belts on the outside of the building, the employer was nevertheless liable as he should have devised a system of work which would have made the work and the premises safe.

3   Safe plant and equipment

An employer is under a duty to provide proper and safe plant and equipment for the work. He must also maintain the equipment in good condition and remedy any known defects. He may incur liability if he fails to provide the appropriate equipment in circumstances where there is an obvious need for such equipment.

In *Lovell v. Blundells & Crompten Co. Ltd*, an employee who was cleaning a ship's boilers needed staging to finish the task, and erected staging with planks he found on the site. The planks were defective and the employee fell and was injured. The employer was held liable as he had failed to provide staging or prescribe a system of working.

An employer will also incur liability if he fails to provide the requisite quantity of equipment required for a particular task. In *Machray v. Stewarts & Lloyds Ltd*, only one block and tackle was available on a site when a very large pipe had to be fixed high above ground. An experienced fitter was injured as a result of the pipe swinging out of control, and the employer was held liable for his injuries.

An employer will be in breach of his duty if he provides plant and equipment which he knows, or ought to have known, was defective. In *Bradford v. Robinson Rentals*, an employer who sent an employee in a van with a defective heater on a round trip of four hundred miles in severe weather, was liable when the employee contracted frostbite.

This duty is not restricted to the provisions of machinery, e.g. in *Bowater v. Rowley Regis Corporation*, an employer was liable for injuries sustained by an employee, when a horse which was known to be prone to bolting, did in fact bolt. In *Naismith v. London Film Productions Ltd*, sacking draped over a film extra caught fire. The employers were held liable for providing dangerous equipment.

An employer cannot avoid liability by claiming that, although he provided the equipment, the fault is attributable to the third party who supplied him with the equipment.

The Employer's Liability (Defective Equipment) Act 1969 provides that if an employee suffers a personal injury in the course of his employment, as a consequence of a defect in the equipment provided by the employer for the purpose of the employer's business, and the defect is attributable to the fault of a third party, the injury shall be deemed to be attributable to the employer's negligence. The employer may, however, bring proceedings against the third party for an indemnity in respect of the damages which he has had to pay to an employee. Equipment includes any plant and machinery, vehicle, aircraft or clothing.

The provisions of this Act give an employee a right of action when he might not have a right at common law. At common law an employer is not liable for a latent defect in the equipment (i.e. a defect which cannot be discovered and remedied by a reasonable inspection), unless the employee can show that the defect could have been discovered and remedied by proper inspection. Prior to the passing of this Act, an employer had a good defence if he could prove that he had used reasonable care in selecting the tool or machine in question, e.g. he had purchased it from a reputable supplier or manufcturer.

An employer will not necessarily incur liability if he fails to provide the latest and safest equipment available for that particular task. It may well be a factor to be taken into account in determining whether there has been negligence on the part of the employer.

4   Competent fellow employees

An employer is obliged to exercise reasonable care in selecting competent employees. He will be vicariously liable for an injury to an employee caused by the negligence of a fellow employee. An employee who fails to prove negligence may be able to claim damages if he can show that the employer was negligent in selecting those employees, whose acttions have caused the injury in question. In *Butler v. Fife Coal Company Ltd*, the widow of a miner killed as a result of a mine explosion was able to prove that the under manager and other responsible mine officials had not evacuated the mine, despite being aware of the presence of gas. The mine owners were therefore liable, as they had failed to appoint and keep in charge persons competent to deal with possible dangers arising at the mine.

The duty extends to the recruitment or the continued employment of individuals who are potentially dangerous, e.g. practical jokers. In *Hudson v. Ridge Manufacturing Co. Ltd*, an employer continued to employ an individual who had been warned on several occasions about indulging in horseplay and skylarking. The employer was held liable for the injuries to an employee caused by the actions of the individual in question.

An employer has a good defence to an action for unfair dismissal if he shows that the reason for the dismissal was the dangerous or potentially dangerous conduct of the employee (see p. 57).

An employer may not be liable if an employee acts in a manner which is alien to his known behaviour and character and injures a fellow employee. In *Coddington v. International Harvester of Great Britain Ltd*, an employee kicked a tin of burning thinners towards an employee, who in the agony of the moment kicked the tin away towards Coddington, who was badly burned when he was enveloped by the flames. The employer was not liable as there had been no indication the first employee's behaviour that he would act in this way, and the act was outside the scope of his employment.

Employee's action for negligence

An employee who has been injured whilst at work will only succeed in an action for negligence against his employer if he can prove (*a*) he was owed a duty of care by the employer, and (*b*) there was a breach of that duty which resulted in the injury.

This is often a difficult task. An employee will also be assisted in the action: if (*a*) he can show that the employer had acted contrary to the normal practice of the particular trade, and (*b*) he can cite *Res ipsa loquitur*. This maxim provides that if an accident is such that it could not have occurred without there being negligence on the part of the person managing or controlling the operation, he must prove that: (*a*) he had exercised all reasonable care; (*b*) the accident was due to some specific cause; and (*c*) he was not negligent.

Sir William Earle CJ in *Scott v. London & St Katherine Docks Co.* stated 'There must be reasonable evidence of negligence, but where the thing is shown to be under the management of the defendant or his servants, and the accident is such as in the ordinary course of things does not happen if those who have the management use proper care, it affords reasonable evidence, in the absence of explanation by the defendant, that the accident arose from want of care'.

In that case six bags of sugar fell on a customs officer when he was passing the defendant's warehouse. It was held that it was for the defendants to rebut the presumption of negligence on their part.

In *Moore v. Fox & Sons*, an employee was killed as a result of a gas explosion. The gas had accumulated under a de-rusting tank which was heated by a gas burner. It was held that the maxim *res ipsa loquitur* applied, and as the defendants had failed to disprove negligence on their part they were liable for damages.

An employee may also be assisted in an action for negligence by certain provisions of the Health and Safety at Work Act 1974.

(i) An employee may show that the employer has not complied with the Code of Practice issued under the Health and Safety at Work Act.

(ii) A health and safety inspector may release any information arising out of any accident or occurrence investigated by him, to a potential litigant.

Under the Employers' Liability (Compulsory Insurance) Act 1969, an employer must take out an insurance policy against liability for bodily injury and disease sustained by his employees and arising out of and in the course of their employment. The policy must provide a minimum cover of £2 000 000 for any one occurrence. An employer, who is not insured, may be fined £500 for each day in default. He must also display a Certificate of Insurance at each place of business.

Employer's defences to an action for negligence

1 Contributory negligence

An employer may allege that, although he was negligent in failing to observe a common law duty, the substantial cause of the accident was the failure of the employee to observe the reasonable degree of care expected in those circumstances. This is known as the doctrine of *contributory negligence.*

If the employer's claim is upheld, the court will estimate the amount that would have been awarded had the employee been blameless, and reduce it 'to such extent as the court thinks just and equitable, having regard to the plaintiff's (employee's) share of the responsibility for the damage' (Law Reform (Contributory Negligence) Act 1945).

The courts must therefore assess: (*a*) the causative potency of the acts of the parties, and (*b*) the degree of blameworthiness to be attached to these acts. The following cases illustrate the working of the rule.

An employer was held liable for not providing a handrail in breach of building regulations. The damages were reduced by fifty per cent as the employee had not disclosed that he was an epileptic and had been advised by his doctor not to work at heights (*Cork v. Kirkby Maclean Ltd*).

An employer did not lock the door to a ventilation shaft and was liable for the injuries sustained by an employee who climbed up the shaft to rescue a bird roosting on machinery. The damages were reduced by ninety percent because of the employee's gross irresponsibility (*Uddin v. Associated Portland Cement Company*).

2   *Volenti non fit injuria*

An employer may plead *volenti non fit injuria* i.e. the employee consented to run the risk of injury. Some occupations are inherently dangerous, e.g. test pilot and deep-sea diver, and an employee engaged in such an occupation, who is aware of the risks involved, may not claim damages from his employer if he suffers injury from his occupation. The pay of such an employee is usually proportional to the risks undertaken and the additional risk payment is generally known as danger money.

However, knowledge of the risks is not synonymous with consent, as an employee is often aware of the risk but does not consent to undertake the risk.

In *Smith v. Baker*, an employee working in a railway cutting was aware that a crane carrying heavy stones often swung its load over his head. No warning was given as to when a load would be swung, and Smith was injured by a stone which fell from the crane. The employer was liable, for although the employee was aware of the risk, there was no evidence to indicate that he had accepted it.

The defence of *volenti non fit injuria* rarely succeeds in employment cases as an employer is under a duty to provide a reasonably safe system of working. Any change in that system which increases the risk to an employee places a greater burden on the employer to prove the employee's acceptance of that risk.

If a statute imposes a duty on an employee and he disregards that duty, the employer is entitled to invoke the defence of *volenti non fit injuria*. In *ICI Ltd v. Shatwell*, statutory regulations laid down that the testing of detonating wires should only be done from a place of shelter when all the persons in the vicinity had withdrawn from the area. One of a team of three shot firers went to obtain a longer cable, and the other two decided to test the circuit in the open. An explosion occurred and the two were injured. As the employers had also issued instructions in accordance with the statutory regulations, they were able to invoke the defence of *volenti non fit injuria*.

3   Employee's conduct

No liability is incurred by an employer if he can prove that the *employee's conduct* was the sole cause of the accident. In *Horne v. Lec Refrigeration Ltd*, a tool-setter was killed when working on a press which was insecurely fenced, contrary to the Factories Act 1961. Despite being in breach of the Factories Act, the employers were held not liable as the sole cause of the accident was the employee's failure to observe the safety drill. In *Boyle v. Kodak Ltd*, an employee fell when climbing a ladder to secure the ladder to an oil storage tank he was painting. The ladder was inside the tank, but he could have secured it by climbing a fixed ladder on the outside of the tank. It was held that the employee alone was to blame for the accident.

4 Remoteness of damage

An employer will not be liable for injuries resulting from circumstances which he could not reasonably have foreseen. The courts have applied the rules of *remoteness of damage*, established in the Wagon Mound case, to this situation. In this case the defendant's employees carelessly spilt oil into Sydney Harbour. The oil was carried by wind and tide to the other side of the harbour and spread alongside the plaintiff's wharf. Welding operations were being carried on at the wharf and sparks fell into the water. The oil caught fire and damaged the plaintiff's wharf and ships that were alongside. It was held that a reasonable man could not have foreseen the consequences of the original spillage of oil.

In *Doughty v. Turner*, an asbestos cover fell into a cauldron of molten metal. The resulting explosion which injured an employee standing nearby was unexpected and unforeseen. As the explosion and the consequent injuries were not reasonably foreseeable, the employer was not liable.

If it is likely that an injury will result from the employer's negligent act, it is immaterial if the type of accident or injury which does in fact occur, is not the one envisaged by the parties, as long as it is reasonably foreseeable that some injury would occur. In *Smith v. Leech Brain*, an employee was burned on the lip by molten metal as a result of the employer's negligence. His lip was in a premalignant condition and the employee developed cancer from the burn, from which he died. The employer was nevertheless held liable for this unexpected consequence.

The Health and Safety at Work Act 1974

The various responsibilities and duties of both the employee and the employer are covered by the Health and Safety at Work Act 1974, which is based on the report of the Royal Commission on Safety and Health at Work which was published in 1972. The Royal Commission was set up in 1970 under the chairmanship of Lord Robens to review industrial safety legislation. The report found that on average a thousand people were killed at work in Britain every year, and about half a million were injured. Twenty-three million working days were lost annually due to industrial accidents and diseases, and the cost in terms of lost production and diverted resources amounted to nearly one per cent of the gross national product. It concluded that the root cause of ill health and accidents at work was apathy.

The report criticised the existing state of the law. It found that nine separate groups of statutes and some five hundred statutory instruments dealt with industrial safety legislation, which was separately administered by five central government departments (Employment, Home Office, Trade and Industry, Environment, and Agriculture) with seven separate inspectorates having responsibility for its enforcement.

The Commission's main proposal was for the enactment of a major statute accompanied by a unified administration with overall responsibility for industrial health and safety legislation. The Report was adopted almost in its entirety and resulted in the Health and Safety at Work Act 1974. Part 1 of the Act deals with health, safety and welfare in connection with work, and with the control of dangerous substances and emissions into the atmosphere. (Only certain aspects of Part 1 are dealt with in the following synopsis.)

The objectives of Part 1 are clearly stated as:

1 Securing the health, safety and welfare of persons at work;
2 Protecting persons other than those at work against risks to their health and safety arising out of or in connection with work activities;
3 Controlling the keeping and use of explosive or highly flammable or otherwise dangerous substances, and generally preventing the unlawful acquisition, possession and use of such substances;

4   Controlling the emission into the atmosphere of noxious or
offensive substances from those premises prescribed by regulations.

The Act established two new bodies to promote its objectives
and to ensure that implementation of its provisions. These are
the Health and Safety Commission and the Health and Safety
Executive.

The HSWA is superimposed on earlier related legislation, e.g.
the Factories Act 1961, the Mines and Quarries Act 1954, and the
Offices, Shops and Railway Premises Act 1963, which also deal with
the health and safety of employees. The parties concerned must
therefore comply with the duties imposed by earlier legislation as
well as with those imposed by the HSWA. The majority of the enforcement provisions of the earlier Acts have been replaced by the
enforcement procedures of the HSWA, which aims ultimately to
replace the earlier regulations by a system of regulations and
approved codes of practice operating in combination with the other
provisions of the HSWA. The new system would maintain or
improve the standards of health safety or welfare established by
earlier legislation.

The Health and Safety Commission
The Health and Safety Commission consists of a chairman and from
six to nine members appointed by the Secretary of State, including
three representing employers and three representing employees.
The Secretary of State must consult both employers and employee's
organisations, local authorities and professional organisations on
the appointment of members.

The Commission's duty is:

1   To assist and encourage compliance with the Act;
2   To encourage and promote research and training;
3   To establish an information and advisory service;
4   To submit proposals to the Government for regulations under
the Act.

The Commission may, with the consent of the Secretary of State,
serve a notice on any person requiring him to provide the Commission with information necessary for carrying out its functions; or
to supply necessary information to an enforcing authority (i.e. the

Health and Safety Executive or its agencies, the local authority) to enable it to exercise its functions.

The Commission may also initiate an inquiry and investigate any accident, occurrence, situation or other matter which the Commission thinks it necessary or expedient to investigate. (This includes the situation where new regulations might be required.) The Commission may at any time direct the Executive or authorise any other person to investigate and report, or direct any inquiry to be held (with the consent of the Secretary of State). Such an inquiry is usually held in public and the regulations dealings with the conduct of inquiries may include provisions which grant to the person conducting the inquiry a power of entry and inspection of premises; a power to summon witnesses or produce documents, and the power to take evidence on oath and administer oaths, or to require the making of declarations.

The Commission may after consultation with the Secretary of State approve and issue codes of practice. It may also approve codes of practice issued by other bodies. Any relevant provision of an approved code of practice is admissible in evidence.

The Health and Safety Executive

The Executive consists of three full-time members who are appointed by the Commission, with the approval of the Secretary of State. The Executive's duty is to exercise on behalf of the Commission any of the Commission's functions which it is asked to carry out, and to make adequate arrangements for the enforcement of legislation.

The Executive's staff includes six Inspectorates (Agriculture, Alikali and Clean Air, Explosives, Factory, Mines and Quarries, and Nuclear Installations), and the Employment Medical Advisory Service.

Duties imposed by the HSWA

The Act imposes duties connected with health and safety at work on a number of persons. Duties are imposed on employers; manufacturers, designers and suppliers of articles and substances; persons in control of premises; and employees.

Employers
The HSWA imposes the following duties on employers.

(a) An employer must provide and maintain plant and systems of work that are, so far as is reasonably practicable, safe and without risks to health.

(b) He must make arrangement for ensuring, so far as is reasonably practicable, the safety and absence of risks to health in using, handling, storing and transporting articles and substances.

(c) He must provide such information, instruction, training and supervision as is necessary to ensure, so far as is reasonably practicable, the health and safety at work of his employees.

(d) He must ensure that, so far as is reasonably practicable, any place of work which is under his control is maintained in a safe condition and does not pose a risk to health. He must also ensure that access to and egress from the work places are safe and without such risks.

(e) He must provide and maintain a working environment for his employees, that is safe, without risks to health, and adequate as regards facilities and arrangements for their welfare at work, so far as is reasonably practicable.

The Act also requires every employer to prepare a written statement of his general safety policy and to bring it to the attention of his employees. This must set out the employer's aims and objectives for improving health and safety at work, and the organisation and arrangements currently in force for achieving these objectives. Employers with fewer than five employees are exempt from these requirements.

Recognised trade unions are given the right to appoint safety representatives to represent the employees in consultations with the employer in matters of health and safety.

An employer also has a duty to conduct his undertakings in such a way to ensure, so far as is reasonably practicable, that persons who are not in his employment, e.g. outside contractors and their workers, visitors and members of the public, are not exposed to risks to their health and safety. In general the standard of care required for those persons is similar to the standard required for the health and safety of employees. A similar duty is imposed upon a self-employed person.

Manufacturers, designers, importers and suppliers

The manufacturers, designers, importers and suppliers of articles and substances for use at work must ensure that so far as is reasonably practicable any article (by virtue of its design and construction) or substance is safe and is without risk to health and safety when properly used.

The article or substance must be tested and examined for the performance of that duty, and adequate information must be available for the use for which an article or substance has been designed or tested. It will not be necessary for a designer, manufacturer, importer or supplier to repeat any tests, examination or research on an article or substance in order to comply with the duties laid down by the Act, if it is reasonable to rely on the results of these tests, examinations or research. If an article or substance is known to be inherently dangerous, information should be readily available regarding any safety precautions to be taken for its handling and storage.

It is the duty of any person who undertakes the design or manufacture of an article or substance for use at work to carry out or arrange for the carrying out of any necessary research with a view to the discovery and, so far as is reasonably practicable, the elimination or minimisation of any risks to health or safety caused by the design of the article or substance.

Any person who erects or installs any article for use at work in any premises must ensure, so far as is reasonably practicable, that nothing about the way in which it is erected or installed makes it unsafe or a health risk.

Persons in control of premises

A person who is in control of premises must use the most practicable means to prevent the emission into the atmosphere from those premises of noxious or offensive substances, and must render harmless and inoffensive such substances as may be emitted. A substance is defined as any natural or artificial substance, whether in solid, liquid or gaseous form.

A person who is in control of non-domestic premises owes certain duties to persons who are not his employees. He must take measures to ensure, so far as is reasonably practicable, that the premises, and any entry or exit from the premises, and any plant or substance in the premises or provided for use there is safe and without risk to health.

These duties apply when any person enters such premises by reason of a contract e.g. a maintenance engineer, and it also applies to premises where machinery or equipment or substances are provided for the use of other persons, e.g. a launderette or a car wash.

Employees

It is the duty of every employee while at work: (*a*) To take reasonable care for the health and safety of himself, and of other persons who may be affected by his acts or omissions at work; and (*b*) to co-operate with his employer or any other person any duty or requirement imposed under any of the relevant statutory provisions. The Act also provides that no person shall intentionally or recklessly interfere with or misuse anything provided in the interests of health, safety or welfare.

Enforcement of the HSWA

Inspectors

Every enforcing authority may appoint suitably qualified persons as inspectors to carry into effect the relevant statutory provisions. Inspectors are given wide powers which include the right:

1 To enter into premises; at any reasonable time (or in a situation which he thinks dangerous at any time);
2 To take with him a constable if he reasonably apprehends any serious obstructions in the execution of this duty;
3 To take with him any other person or any equipment or material on entering premises;
4 To make such examination and investigations as may be necessary;
5 To direct that any premises which he has power to enter shall be left undisturbed for the purposes of any examination or investigation;

6 To take such measurements and photographs and make such recordings as he considers necessary;

7 To take samples of any articles or substances or the atmosphere in the premises;

8 To dismantle or subject to any process or test any article or substance found on the premises which appears to have caused or to be likely to cause danger to health and safety;

9 To question any person whom he has reasonable cause to believe may be able to give any information relevant to any examination or investigation;

10 To require the production of, inspect, and take a copy of any books or documents required to be kept by a relevant statutory provision or which is necessary to see for the purposes of any examination or investigation;

11 To require any person to afford him such facilities and assist-ance with respect to any matters or things within that person's control or in relation to that person's responsibilities as are necessary to enable the inspector to exercise the powers granted to him;

12 Any other right necessary for carrying out any of the previously listed powers.

An inspector must not disclose information obtained by him by virtue of his powers, except in the following circumstances:

(*a*) For the purposes of his functions; or

(*b*) For the purposes of any legal proceedings or any investigation or inquiry held under the direction of the Health and Safety Commission or Executive, or for the purposes of a report of any such proceedings or inquiry of a special report made by virtue of such a directive;

(*c*) With the relevant consent of a person who furnished the information in pursuance of an inspector's examination or investigation; or having responsibilities in relation to the premises where the information was obtained;

(*d*) When it is necessary to assist in keeping persons or their representatives, (e.g. safety representatives) employed at any premises adequately informed about matters affecting their health, safety and welfare. He must inform these persons as to any factual information obtained by him relating to these premises and any action which he has taken or proposes to take in connection with these premises. Any information given to employees must also be given to the employer.

Improvement and prohibition notices

If an inspector is of the opinion that a person is contravening health and safety legislation, or has in the past contravened such legislation in circumstances that it is likely that he will do so again, the inspector may serve an *improvement notice* on that person. This requires him to remedy the contravention or the matters occasioning it within whatever period may be specified in the notice.

If an inspector is of the opinion that the activities which are being, or about to be carried on by a person involve, or will involve a risk of personal injury he may serve a *prohibition notice* on that person. The notice may be deferred, in which case it will specify the remedial measures to be taken and fix a time after which the work will be prohibited; or it may take immediate effect in which case the work activity must cease immediately. An inspector will issue an immediate prohibition notice where he is of the opinion that there is an immediate risk of injury.

A person on whom a notice is served may appeal to an industrial tribunal, within twenty-one days of the issue of the notice. The appeal may challenge the inspector's views regarding the contravention of legislation, the risk of personal injury, the time limit in the notice, or the remedial measures specified in the notice.

Safety representatives

The Act provides for the appointment in prescribed cases of safety representatives who will represent the employees in consultations with the employer. The Safety Representatives and Safety Committes Regulations 1977 became operative on 1 October 1978 and were accompanied by a Code of Practice. The Health and Safety Commission issues guidance notes on the operation of the consultative system.

Only recognised trade unions have the right to appoint safety representatives. The Regulations do not specify the number of representatives that may be appointed, but guidance notes do indicate the criteria to be adopted and suggest that the following factors should be taken into consideration:

1   The total number of employees and their occupations;
2   The size of the work place and the type of work conducted;
3   The shift system and the degree and character of any inherent dangers.

The representatives' functions are set out in the Regulations.

(*a*)   To investigate potential hazards and dangerous occurrences at the work place and to examine the causes of accidents at the work place;
(*b*)   To investigate complaints by an employee he represents relating to that employee's health, safety or welfare at work;
(*c*)   To make representations to the employer on matters of health, safety and welfare;
(*d*)   To carry out inspections;
(*e*)   To represent the employees in consultations with the various inspectors and enforcement authorities;
(*f*)   To receive information from inspectors;
(*g*)   To attend meetings of safety committees.

An employer should permit a safety representative to take time off with pay during the employee's working hours in order to perform these functions. Safety representatives are entitled to inspect the work place, if they have given the employer written notice of their intention to inspect. Inspection can only be made at three-monthly intervals, unless the employer agrees to more frequent inspections, or these has been a sustantial change in conditions of work, or new information on hazards has been published by the Health and Safety Commission. Inspections may also be carried out where there has been a notifiable accident or dangerous occurrence in a work place, or a notifiable disease has been contracted, and the employees' interests are involved. Representatives are also entitled to inspect and take copies of any relevant documents. An employer must establish a safety committee if requested to do so in writing by at least two safety representatives. The committee must be established within three months of the written request.

A breach of the provisions of the HSWA is a criminal offence which may render the offender liable to a sentence of up to two years' imprisonment and/or a fine for an unlimited amount. A person who has been convicted of contravening an improvement or prohibition order, or an order of a court is liable to a fine of up to £100 for each day he continues to ignore that order.

The Act provides that there is no right of civil action for an injury which results from a failure to comply with the general duties laid down in Part 1 of the Act. This does not affect to any right of action which exists apart from the Act. A breach of any duty imposed by health and safety regulations is actionable unless the regulations state otherwise.

6

Wages

An employer is under a contractual obligation to pay wages to his employees, whether the contract of employment is in writing or merely a verbal agreement. He is also under an obligation to supply each employee, within thirteen weeks of the commencement of employment, with written particulars of the terms of his employment (EPCA, section 1). These particulars include:

1 The scale or rate of remuneration or the method of calculating remuneration;
2 The intervals at which remuneration is paid, i.e. whether weekly or monthly or by some other period;
3 Any terms and conditions, relating to:
    (*a*) entitlement to holidays, including public holidays, and holiday pay;
    (*b*) incapacity for work due to sickness or injury including any provision for sick pay;
    (*c*) pensions and pension schemes.

An employee is also entitled under section 8 of the EPCA to an itemised pay statement which contains:

1 The gross amount of the wages or salary;
2 The amount of any variable or fixed deduction made from the gross amount and the purpose for which it is made;
3 The net amount of wages or salary payable;
4 The amount and method of each part payment where different parts of the net amount are paid in different ways.

In the absence of written particulars, the court will usually imply a term in an employee's contract of employment that he should be paid a reasonable sum for his services i.e. on a *quantum meruit* basis (as much as he had earned). In *Way v. Latilla*, the plaintiff claimed that the defendant had agreed to pay him a reasonable sum for information and reports relating to gold mines and concessions in West Africa. It was held that a contract existed which indicated that the work was not gratuitous. In view of the defendant's profits of £1 000 000, the plaintiff was held to be entitled to £5000 on a *quantum meruit* basis.

In *Powell v. Braun*, an employer offered to pay his secretary a bonus, based on the net trading profits of the business, in lieu of an increase in salary. The method of calculating the bonus was never agreed. Nevertheless it was held that such a bonus was payable on a *quantum meruit* basis.

However, in *Re Richmond Gate Property Co. Ltd*, it was held that a managing director was not entitled to payment for the nine months prior to the company's liquidation. He was to be paid 'such remuneration as the directors may determine'. As there was a mechanism for determining his remuneration, he was not entitled to claim on a *quantum meruit* basis. The directors had not determined the amount of his remuneration, and consequently he was not entitled to any payment.

Wages and salaries in certain employments may fluctuate according to the number of hours worked and the degree of productivity attained. Certain employees are paid on a piecework basis, or an hourly basis. Other employees are given a bonus or a commission in lieu of, or in addition to, their wages. It is important in the context of modern employment legislation to determine 'a week's pay', and the basis of its calculation, in order to determine the amount of compensation for unfair dismissal, redundancy and guarantee payments.

Calculation of a week's pay

An employee's entitlement to various payments under employment statutes (e.g. redundancy payments, maternity payments, compensation for unfair dismissal) is based on a formula which includes the amount of a week's pay as one of the main factors. Schedule 14 of the EPCA sets out the method of calculating normal working hours and hence a week's pay. It is sometimes necessary to ascertain an employee's working hours before it is possible to calculate a week's pay. The rules are as follows:

1   If there are normal working hours and the employee's remuneration does not vary with the amount of work done in the period, a week's pay is the amount payable by the employer on the calculation date.

2   If there are normal working hours, but the employee's remuneration varies with the amount of work done, or the hours of work vary from week to week, a week's pay is calculated at the average hourly rate paid over the previous twelve-week period, ending on the calculation date.

3   If normal working hours are not worked, a week's pay is the amount of the employee's average weekly remuneration over the previous twelve-week period, ending on the calculation date.

4   Overtime will only be included as part of an employee's normal working hours when an employer is under an obligation to provide a fixed period of overtime, and an employee is under an obligation to work this period of overtime, in addition to a fixed number of compulsory working hours.

5   In calculating an employee's remuneration, certain benefits, e.g. travelling allowances and accommodation are disregarded, but bonuses and commissions may be included in the computation, taking $12/13$ of a quarterly bonus or $12/52$ of an annual bonus.

Method of payment

Truck Acts
The basic rule is that a manual worker must be paid his full wage in current coin of the realm. This originates from the Truck Act of 1831, which prohibited the practice of trucking, i.e. the payment of wages in tokens or checks which could only be exchanged for goods at a local store, or one owned by the factory or mine owner. Although most of the sections of this, the first Truck Act, have been repealed, certain sections are still in force and relevant today.

The Act relates to the payment of wages of artificers and provides that 'the entire amount of the wages earned by or payable to any artificer . . . in respect of any labour by him done . . . shall be actually paid . . . in the current coin of this realm, not otherwise'. This has since been amended by the Payment of Wages Act 1960, and certain deductions are now permitted, as every taxpayer and insurance contributor realises. Nevertheless, any deductions outside those permitted will contravene the Truck Acts and will be 'illegal, null and void'.

The Truck Act of 1831 applied to the wages of artificers. A later Act decreed that the term *artificer* should include workmen (Truck Amendment Act 1887). The term *workmen* has been recently defined as including a labourer, servant in husbandry, journeyman, artificer, handicraftman, miner, or any person otherwise engaged in manual labour working under a contract for an employer. It does not include a seaman or a domestic or manual servant (Statute Law (Repeals) Act 1973).

A considerable number of cases have been heard by the courts to determine whether a particular class of work is substantially manual employment. A bus driver who maintained his vehicle, and a foreman engaged in manual labour who hired and paid his assistants, were both held to be workmen engaged in manual labour. However, a bus conductor was held not to be so engaged, as it was his primary function to invite passengers to enter the bus and to take fares on his employer's behalf. The guard of a freight train was held not to be engaged in manual labour, while a potman living in a public house was held to be a domestic servant.

In *Kenyon v. Darwen Cotton Manufacturing Co.*, a company's employees purchased shares from the company, in order to assist the company during a period of trade recession. Payment was made by weekly deductions from their pay packet. It was nevertheless held to be a contravention of the Truck Acts, as it amounted to payment of part of their wages in shares and not in cash.

It was established in *Hewlett v. Allen* that a payment made to a third party (in this case a sick and accident club), by the employer on the employee's behalf and at the employee's written request, and later deducted from the employee's wages, is the equivalent of a constructive payment to the employee. However, such deductions must be made to settle obligations with a third party and not with the employer. Many employers, in conjunction with the union and the workman concerned, deduct union subscriptions at source from the workman's pay. This 'check-off' is legal as long as details of deductions are given to the employee in his itemised pay statement.

In *Penman v. Fife Coal Co. Ltd*, an employee agreed in writing to deductions being made from his wages by his employer to pay arrears of rent owed by his father, a former company employee, who was threatened with eviction. It was held that such deductions contravened the Truck Acts.

An employer may make deductions from a workman's wages in respect of certain items if there is a written agreement to that effect, signed by the workman. These items are:

1 The supply of medicine or medical attendance or fuel;
2 The supply of tools or implements to miners;
3 The supply of hay, corn or provender to any beast of burden used by any workman;
4 The supply of food prepared and consumed on the employer's premises (the precise wording of the Act is 'the supplying . . . to any such artificer any victuals dressed on prepared under the roof of any such employer and there consumed by such artificer');
5 The letting of a tenement to his workman.

The amount of the deductions must not exceed the true value of the goods supplied, or of the services rendered by the employer.

An employer may also advance money for the education of a workman's child or children, and may deduct these sums from wages, as long as the employee's written consent is obtained. Money may also be advanced by an employer to pay the workman's contributions to any friendly society or bank for saving, or for the relief of a workman in sickness, but these advances may not be deducted from the workman's wages.

The Truck Amendment Act 1887 makes special provisions for a servant in husbandry (e.g. farm labourer), and states that it shall not be illegal to give such a workman 'food, drink, not being intoxicating, a cottage, or other allowances or privileges in addition to money wages as a remuneration for his services'. This Act also provides that whenever by agreement or custom or otherwise, a workman is entitled to receive an advance of his wages, it is unlawful for an employer to withhold such an advance or make any charge in respect of it.

The Truck Act 1896 permits an employer to make deductions or impose a fine in respect of any bad or negligent work by a workman. The workman must have either agreed in writing to a deduction or fine, or the employer must have posted a notice containing the terms of the contract, in a prominent place accessible to the workman, where it may be easily seen, read and be copied.

Any deduction or fine must not exceed the actual or estimated damage or loss and must be fair and reasonable in all the circumstances. Details of such a fine and deduction must be given in writing to the employee.

Employees in certain industries are paid according to the weight or measure of substances or materials produced or handled by them, e.g. coal mining; production of iron and steel, cement and lime; loading or unloading of goods from ships and barges. Under the Mines and Quarries Act 1954, and the Checkweighing in Various Industries Act 1919, these employees may, at their own expense, appoint a checkweigher to supervise such weighing or measuring, in order to determine correctly the amounts to be paid and the deductions to be made.

Payments of Wages Act
The Payments of Wages Act 1960 modifies the Truck Acts in that an employer may, at the written request of an employee, pay his employee's wages other than in coin of the realm. Payment may be made into an employee's bank account, or a named joint account; by postal order, money order, or by cheque. A cheque must name the employee as the payee and the employer may not make a deduction from the employee's wages to cover the expense. Either party may give written notice of their intention to cancel the agreement and this will take effect at the end of four weeks.

If an employee is absent from his place of employment, either in connection with his employment or due to illness or sustaining personal injury, his wages may be paid by postal or money order without his prior agreement. If an employee has given written notice to the employer that he does not wish to be paid in this way in these circumstances, the employer may not make use of these provisions.

Attachment of earnings

An employer may be instructed by a court to make deductions from an employee's wages under the terms of an attachment order. The Attachment of Earnings Act 1971 allows an order to be made in:

The High Court, to secure payments under a High Court maintenance order.

A County Court, to secure payments under a High Court, or County Court, maintenance order; under an administration order; or to settle a judgment debt of over £5.

A Magistrates' Court for a Magistrates' Court maintenance order, the payment of a fine, and any legal aid contribution.

The employer must deduct the amounts specified from the employee's earnings and pay these to the specified collecting officer—usually a High Court officer, the County Court Registrar, or a Magistrates' Clerk. He must also inform the appropriate court, within ten days, if the employee leaves his service. The court must, however, specify a rate of protected earnings. Should an employee's earnings fall below this norm, no deductions can be paid from his wages.

An employer must, on each occasion when a deduction is made, inform the employee in writing of the amount of the deduction, and may charge 5p for administrative expenses.

An employer must give particulars of an employee's actual or estimated future earnings when requested to do so by the court. He will be liable to a fine of £25 if he fails to comply with the court's request.

Suspension

An employer may suspend an employee without pay if this right is reserved in the contract of employment. Otherwise an employee is entitled to damages for loss of earnings during the period of suspension. In *Hanley v. Pease*, an employee suspended without pay for one day was awarded damages equivalent to a day's pay, as on that particular day he was not given the opportunity to earn a day's pay, and the employer's right to suspend him was not reserved in his contract of employment.

If an employer has reserved the right of suspension in the contract, e.g. in the rule book, there is no breach of contract if an employee is suspended without pay and there is no contravention of the Truck Acts.

Pay during suspension on medical grounds

An employee who is suspended from work by his employer on medical grounds, as a result of certain statutory requirements or the provisions of a code of practice issued under the HSWA 1974, is entitled to a maximum of twenty-six weeks' pay during his period of suspension. The employee must have been continuously employed for 4 weeks before the commencement of the suspension.

An employee will be regarded as suspended as long as he continues to be employed by his employer and is not provided with work, or does not perform the work he normally performed before the suspension.

He is not entitled to payment if:

1   He is incapable of work because of disease or physical or mental disablement; or
2   The employer has offered suitable alternative work for that day which the employee has unreasonably refused; or
3   The employee does not comply with reasonable requirements imposed by his employer with a view to ensuring that his services are available.

Guarantee payments

An employee who is not provided with work by his employer is entitled to guarantee payments in respect of a certain number of 'workless' days. The 'workless' days must be due to a diminution in the requirements of the employer's business for work of the kind which the employee is employed to do; or to any other occurrence affecting the normal working of the employer's business in relation to work of the kind which the employee is employed to do.

An employee is entitled to guarantee payments for up to five days in any quarter. The maximum entitlement is £9.40 a day, and an employee must be continuously employed for four weeks before the day on which the claim is made.

An employee is not entitled to a guarantee payment if:

1   The failure to provide work occurs as a consequence of a trade dispute involving any employee of his employer or an associated employer; or
2   The employer has offered suitable alternative work for that day which the employee has unreasonably refused; or
3   The employee does not comply with reasonable requirements imposed by his employer with a view to ensuring that his services are available.

Sick pay

An employee must be given written particulars of any entitlement to wages during sickness. This is one of the items which must be included in the document outlining the terms of his contract.

An individual's contract of employment may contain provisions dealing with an entitlement to sick pay, or reference may be made in the contract to a collective agreement, whose terms will then be incorporated into the individual's contract. An employer is under no obligation to provide for the payment of sick pay. The only exception is that an employee who has been given notice and 'is incapable of work because of sickness or injury' must be paid by his employer during the period of notice.

If there is no specific provision dealing with sick pay, a term will not necessarily be implied that payment will be made by the employer during a period of sickness. All the facts and circumstances must be considered to establish whether such a term should be implied. Factors to consider are the customs and practice in the industry, and the knowledge and actions of the parties. In *Mears v. Safecar Security Ltd*, an employee was absent from work for a total of seven months out of his fourteen-month period of employment. There was no reference to sick pay in his written contract, and he did not apply for wages during his periods of absence, having been told by his fellow employees that sick pay was not provided. It was held that in these circumstances there was no entitlement to sick pay from his employer.

Sick pay and sickness benefit are discussed in detail in Chapter 14.

Equal pay

The Equal Pay Act 1970 outlaws discrimination 'as regards terms and conditions of employment, between men and women'. This Act did not come into force until December 1975, so that employers would have sufficient time to comply with its provisions. By this time its provisions had been substantially amended by the Sex Discrimination Act 1975 (the fully amended provisions of the Equal Pay Act are contained in a schedule to the Sex Discrimination Act).

The question of equal pay had been mooted and examined in this country for over half a century. First examined in 1919, it was reconsidered by a Royal Commission which sat between 1944 and 1946. The British Government was pledged to introduce equal pay legislation, having accepted a Recommendation to Convention 100 of the International Labour Organisation. This provided that each member state should 'promote and . . . ensure the application to all workers of the principle of equal remuneration for men and women to work of equal value.'

The Equal Pay Act provides that if the terms of a contract under which a woman is employed at an establishment in Great Britain do not include, either directly or impliedly, an equality clause, such a clause will be deemed to be included. The provisions of the Act apply equally to men and women. The equality clause operates:

(a)   Where the woman is employed on like work with a man; or
(b)   Where the woman is employed on work rated as equivalent with that of a man in the same employment; or
(c)   Where the woman is employed on work which is in terms of the demands made on her of equal value to that of a man in the same employment (Equal Pay (Amendment) Regulations 1983).

Like work

A woman is regarded as employed on *like work* with men if the work is 'the same or of a broadly similar nature, and the differences . . . are not of practical importance in relation to the terms and conditions of employment'.

In *Capper Pass v. Lawton*, the Appeal Tribunal stated that a two-stage enquiry should be adopted to determine whether people were engaged in like work. A tribunal should firstly adopt a broad approach to determine whether the work is similar, without minutely examining the differences between the work. Secondly if the work is determined broadly similar, a tribunal must then consider whether the differences are of practical importance. In the case in question, a female cook who prepared between 10 and 20 lunches for the firm's directors claimed pay parity with two assistant chefs, who catered for around 350 lunches in the works' canteen. Her work was unsupervised while the assistant chefs worked longer hours under supervision. Despite the minor differences it was held that the work was of a similar nature, involving similar culinary skills and expertise and therefore she was entitled to equal pay.

In *Eaton v. Nuttall*, and *Capper Pass v. Allan*, it was held that additional responsibilities allocated to male employees amounted to differences which were of practical importance. In the first case, a female despatcher was not paid the same rates as her male counterpart. She handled a large number of goods of small value, while he dealt with a small number of goods of high value. As an error on his part would have far more serious financial consequences than an error on the part of the female despatcher, he was entitled to a higher rate of pay.

In the second case, a female canteen employee claimed parity with a male canteen employee, who received an additional shift differential and productivity payment. The additional payments were held to be justified as he was also responsible for stock control and for handling substantial sums of money.

The fact that a male employee works different hours to a female employee does not justify a different rate of pay, if the work is similar. An employer may compensate for unsocial hours, night and weekend work by paying special premiums, and as long he pays the same basic rates to both sexes he does not infringe the provisions of the Act. In *Dugdale v. Kraft Foods*, a female employee was held to be entitled to the same basic rate as her male counterparts, who were obliged to work night shifts, despite the fact that women were debarred from working on night shifts by the provisions of the Factories Act 1961.

When making a comparison, a tribunal must have regard to the frequency or otherwise with which any differences occur in practice, as well as to the nature and extent of these differences. In *Coomes (Holdings) Ltd v. Shields*, a male employee in a betting shop was paid higher hourly rate than his female counterpart. The employers contended that the extra payment was justified as the man's physical presence was a deterrent to potential troublemakers. It was held that the woman was entitled to equal pay as there was no evidence of past trouble, or that the man was specifically trained to deal with troublemakers. In *Ford v. Weston (Chemists) Ltd*, a female dispensary manager claimed equal pay with a male branch manager, as she occasionally deputised for him in his absence. It was held that as these absences were infrequent she was not entitled to equal pay.

Work rated as equivalent

A woman is to be regarded as employed on work rated as equivalent with that of any man in both jobs have been given an equal value in terms of the demands made upon a worker (under such headings as effort, skill and decision-making) under a job evaluation scheme conducted within the undertaking, or within a group of undertakings.

When a job evaluation scheme has been conducted which evaluates a woman's job as equal to a man's, the firm must then modify the terms of the employee's contract to implement the terms of the Equal Pay Act (*O'Brien v. Sim-Chem*). A job evaluation exercise is regarded as conclusive, unless it can be shown that the scheme set 'different values for men and women'.

In *Arnold v. Beecham Group*, the employers had undertaken two job evaluation studies in 1978 and 1980. The employers used the 1980 study to reach agreement on the boundaries of job grades, and the applicant was bracketed with a man as grade 2. There was such an objection to the scheme amongst the supervisors that the 1980 pay settlement was finally agreed upon on the basis of the 1978 scheme, with certain modifications. It was nevertheless held that as there had been a complete study, the applicant was entitled to equal pay. See also Chapter 10.

Work of equal value

A woman (or man) may claim equal pay for work of equal value where a job evaluation scheme has not been carried out. The results of a job evaluation scheme may also be challenged. Industrial tribunals may appoint independent experts to assess whether a woman's job is of equal value to that of a man. An employer may by way of defence rely on matters that go beyond personal differences between the woman and the man with whom she is compared.

Protected rates of pay

Problems have arisen in deciding whether the payment of an employee at a *protected rate*, i.e. at a higher rate than his fellow employees, is a genuine material difference. This situation may occur when an employee's job is down-graded, but he is offered a lower grade job at his previous rate as an alternative to redundancy, or when an industrial injury makes it necessary for an employee to do lighter work, but he is paid at his previous higher rates. This is also known as *red circling* i.e. a red circle around the employee's name on a pay roll signifies that his rate of pay is protected.

An employer seeking to justify a protected payment as a material difference must show that the protected rate is genuine and that 'its origin was not discriminatory'. In *Snoxell v. Vauxhall Motors*, male inspectors were paid at a higher rate than female inspectors, although both groups undertook similar work. The male inspectors were originally part of a male group who received higher wages. As a result of a pay revision, they were re-graded and 'red-circled' until the group was phased out. It was held that the female inspectors were entitled to pay parity.

The payment of a male employee at a higher rate than his female counterpart, for reasons connected with his employment, e.g. market forces, is not regarded as a genuine material difference. In *Fletcher v. Clay Cross (Quarry Services) Ltd*, a male clerk was appointed to fill a vacancy which was advertised as open to persons of either sex. He was paid more than a female employee engaged on like work as he was earning more in his previous employment. It was held that the payment of a higher salary to induce a person to take a job was not a genuine material difference.

Genuine material differences

An equality clause will not operate in cases where an employer is able to prove that, on the balance of probabilities, the variation in terms and conditions is genuinely due to material differences other than sex. This is so, even if an employee has made out a *prima facie* case for equal pay. The difference must be a factor not previously considered when comparing the work of both sexes.

In *Kerr v. Lister and Co.*, both men and women who worked on the night shift were paid at a higher rate than the women working on the day shift. The difference was therefore a difference between day and night rates, not a difference that was attributable to sex.

However, in *Coyne v. Exports Credit Guarantee Department*, a woman's contract provided that any maternity leave should count against normal sick leave allowance. It was held that the leave provisions were therefore less favourable than those granted to a man in like work, and restricted sickness rights, rather than granting maternity rights. It was therefore not a material difference, but due to the sex of the parties, and the contract had to be modified.

In *Albion Shipping Agency v. Arnold*, a woman took over the running of an office at a substantially lower salary than her male predecessor, who was made redundant following a reduction in the volume of business and profits. It was held that although she was employed on like work, the reduction in the volume of business could amount to a material difference other than that of sex.

Other grounds which have been held to be material differences, and therefore justifying different rates of pay for the same work, include the following:

1 Full-time work as opposed to part-time (*Jenkins v. Kingsgate*);
2 Employment in London, as opposed to employment in the provinces (*NAAFI v. Varley*);
3 Skill, capacity and experience of male clerks in an insurance firm (*National Vulcan Engineering Insurance Group v. Wade*);
4 The age and ill health of a former engineer who filled a clerical post (*Methven v. Cow Industrial Polymers*);
5 Extra responsibility, as a result of greater experience of women communications operators (*Avon and Somerset Police Authority v. Emery*).

Article 119

As a member of the European Community, the United Kingdom is bound by the provisions of the Treaty of Rome. Article 119 is of particular importance in this context as it provides that 'men and women should receive equal pay for equal work'. Pay is defined as 'the ordinary basic or minimum wage or salary and any other consideration, whether in cash or in kind, which the worker receives, either directly or indirectly, in respect of his employment from his employer'.

The European Court has recently considered the meaning of 'pay' in two different cases. In *Warringham and Humphreys v. Lloyds Bank*, the Bank required all its clerical officers to join the company's pension schemes. The women's scheme was non-contributory until the age of twenty-five, while the men's scheme was contributory throughout. The employer paid the men an additional sum to compensate for their contributions. It was held that this additional sum constituted pay within the meaning of Article 119. The female employees were entitled to be paid the same contributions as they would have received had they been male employees employed on like work.

In *Garland v. British Rail Engineering Ltd*, a female employee of British Rail Engineering claimed parity of treatment for retired female employees with retired male employees. Both male and female employees were granted concessionary rail travel for themselves, their spouses and children during their working life. On retirement the concession was withdrawn from the families of former female employees, but was still granted to the families of former male employees. The European Court ruled that travel facilities granted to employees after retirement are 'pay' within the meaning of Article 119.

A woman may compare her work with that of a male employee formerly employed in the same post by the same employer. The principle of equal pay is not confined to situations in which men and women are contemporaneously doing equal work for the same employer. In *McCarthy v. Smith*, a man was paid £60 a week as a stockroom manager. On his departure the post was left vacant for four months, when a woman was appointed to the post at a salary of £50 per week. As the duties were similar, it was held that under the principle in Article 119, she should receive equal pay for the same work as her predecessor.

Article 119 defines equal pay in the following terms. '*Equal pay*' without discrimination based on sex means (*a*) that pay for the same work at piece rates shall be calculated on the basis of the same unit of measurement, and (*b*) that pay for work at time rates shall be the same for the same job.

Two directives of the Council of the European Community have extended the 'principle of equal pay' in Article 119 to include 'work to which equal value is attributed' (Directive 75/117) and 'working conditions' (Directive 76/207). The European Court in *Jenkins v. Kingsgate Clothing Productions* held that Directive 75/117 is designed to facilitate the practical application of Article 119. In no way does it alter the scope or the content of the Article.

The Court decided in that case that Article 119 is directly applicable in Member States where the form of the discrimination is one which may be identified solely with the aid of the criteria of equal work and equal pay referred to by the Article. National or Community measures are not required to define these criteria with greater precision in order for them to apply.

Maternity pay

An employee who is absent from work wholly or partly due to pregnancy or confinement will be entitled to maternity pay, as long as certain conditions are fulfilled:

1 She must be an employee.
2 She has continued to be employed by her employer until immediately before the beginning of the eleventh week before the expected week of confinement.
3 She has (at the beginning of the eleventh week) been continuously employed for a period of not less than two years.
4 She informs her employer at least twenty-one days before her absence begins (or as soon as reasonably practicable) that she will be (or is) absent from work wholly or partly due to pregnancy or confinement.
5 She is employed for a minimum of sixteen hours per week. If she has been employed for more than five years, she will be able to claim if she is employed for more than eight hours a week.
6 She must produce a medical certificate stating the expected week of her confinement, if requested to do so by her employer.

Maternity pay is payable for the first six weeks of absence, starting on or falling after the beginning of the eleventh week before the expected week of confinement. An employee is entitled to 9/10 of a week's pay, less the amount of maternity allowance payable, whether or not there is an entitlement to this allowance.

An employee may present a complaint to an industrial tribunal that her employer has failed to pay her the whole or any part of her entitlement to maternity pay. A complaint must be presented before the end of a three-month period, beginning with the last day of the payment period. A tribunal may order the employer to pay the employee the amount of maternity pay which it finds is due to her.

If an employer is insolvent, or refuses to pay the maternity pay due to the employee, she may apply to the Secretary of State who will pay her the due amount from the Maternity Pay Fund. The Secretary of State may then recover from the employer such an amount as he considers reasonable, but this must not exceed the amount which the employer failed to pay. Employers may claim a rebate for the full amount of maternity payments from the Maternity Pay Fund.

Employer's insolvency

If an employer is insolvent, an employee's unpaid wages or salary will be treated as a preferential debt, up to a limit of £800, for the four months preceding the insolvency (Companies Act 1948, section 319; Bankruptcy Act 1914, section 33). *Wages* include holiday pay, sick pay, and, by section 122 of the EPCA, any amounts owed by an employer in respect of: a guarantee payment, remuneration during suspension on medical grounds, payment for time off, and remuneration under a protective award. A preferential creditor is given priority over an ordinary creditor.

The EPCA gives an employee additional rights in that he may recover certain amounts owing to him from the Redundancy Fund. These are:

1 Up to eight weeks arrears of pay;
2 Any amount which the employer is liable to pay during the minimum period of notice required by the EPCA;
3 Up to six weeks' holiday pay entitlement for the twelve months preceding insolvency;

4 Any basic award of compensation for unfair dismissal;

5 Any reasonable sum by way of reimbursement of the whole or part of any fee or premium paid by an apprentice or articled clerk.

Pay also includes amounts owed by an employer under the provisions of section 122 of the EPCA (see above). The maximum amount payable in respect of any week is £145.

Payments may also be made out of the Redundancy Fund where an insolvent employer has failed to pay all the contributions to an occupational pension scheme.

An employee may complain to an industrial tribunal if the Secretary of State fails to make a payment, or a payment made by the Secretary is less than the amount which should have been paid. The industrial tribunal may make a declaration that the Secretary of State ought to make a specified payment.

An employee should first claim as a preferential creditor from his employer's assets. If these are insufficient to meet the employee's claim, he should then apply to the Redundancy Fund under the provisions of S121 of the EPCA. If his claim also exhausts these statutory rights, he will rank as an ordinary creditor in respect of any outstanding amounts.

Wages Councils

Wages, holidays, and other conditions of employment are determined in certain industries by Wages Councils or Statutory Joint Industrial Councils. These bodies have been established in industries where employees are without an effective body to undertake negotiations on their behalf, e.g. retailing, and hotel and catering. This is mainly due to weak, ineffective or non-existent trade union representation in that particular industry. The law governing Wages Councils has been consolidated in the Wages Councils Act 1979.

An order establishing a Wages Council may be made by the Secretary of State for Employment in the following circumstances:

(*a*) If he is of the opinion that adequate machinery does not exist for the remuneration of the employees described in the order.

(*b*) If he gives effect to a recommendation of ACAS that a Wages Council should be established, as a result of an application by a

Joint Industrial Council or other body representing employers or employees, who habitually take part in wage negotiations.

(c) If he gives effect to a recommendation of ACAS following his own reference to ACAS. (If he considers that machinery does not exist, or is inadequate, or is likely to cease to exist he may refer to ACAS the question of whether a Wages Council should be established.)

A Wages Council consists of not more than three individuals, appointed by the Secretary of State as independent persons, and persons representing employers and employees. One of the independent persons will be appointed as Chairman. The Council may make an order dealing with remuneration, holidays, and certain other terms and conditions.

A Wages Council may be converted to a Statutory Joint Industrial Council, at the option of the Secretary of State. It has similar powers to a Wages Council, but its constitution differs in that it has no independent members. The creation of a Statutory Joint Industrial Council is regarded as a natural progression towards free collective bargaining.

Fair Wages Resolution

The government ensures that all employers who are in receipt of government contracts pay fair wages to their employees. The latest in a series of Fair Wages Resolutions was passed by the House of Commons in 1946. It instructs every government department entering into a contract with a private contractor to insert a clause which ensures that:

1 The contractor will pay rates of wages and observe hours and conditions of labour no less favourable than those established for the trade or industry in the district where the work is carried out.

2 In the absence of any local rates of wages, hours or conditions of labour, the contractor will pay rates of wages and observe hours and conditions of labour no less favourable than those observed by other employers in the trade or industry in which the contractor is engaged.

3 The contractor will, in respect of all his employees (whether

employed on the government contract or not) comply with the terms of the resolution.

4   Any disputes as to compliance with the resolution will be referred to the Secretary of State for Employment.

5   The contractor will recognise the freedom of his employees to be members of Trade Unions.

6   The contractor will display a copy of the resolution in every factory, workshop, or place occupied or used by him for the execution of the contract.

7   The contractor will be responsible for ensuring that any sub-contractor employed by him complies with the resolution.

7

Termination of Employment

A contract of employment may be terminated by one of the parties to the contract giving notice to the other. Most employment contracts contain provisions dealing with the length of notice required to be given by either party to bring the contract to an end. In some cases custom or practice in a particular trade or industry may determine the length of the notice required.

A contract may also be terminated by mutual agreement of the parties, with each party releasing the other party from his contractual obligations. Although the majority of employment contracts are terminated by giving the appropriate period of notice, there are certain circumstances when this does not occur. There are four situations to consider:

1 Where the contract is terminated by giving notice;
2 Where the contracted is frustrated, i.e. when the original nature of the contract has undergone a fundamental change;
3 The position of partnership and company employees;
4 Where an employee claims that the employer is in breach of contract by not giving the required period of notice, i.e. he claims there has been a wrongful dismissal.

Notice

In the absence of a provision, custom or agreement, either party is entitled to a reasonable period of notice. What is reasonable depends on a variety of factors, e.g. the employee's position, seniority, length of service, rates and frequency of pay (weekly, monthly, quarterly, annually). A chief engineer of a liner and a newspaper editor have been held to be entitled to twelve months' notice, a company director to three months' notice, a chorus girl to two weeks' notice and a hairdresser's assistant to one week's notice.

These requirements are subject to the minimum periods of entitlement, provided for by the EPCA (see page 101). Any periods of entitlement contained in the contract will be binding on the parties, as long as the terms exceed the statutory minimum. Either party may waive his right to notice, or accept a payment in lieu of notice (EPCA, section 49.3). The acceptance of wages in lieu of notice would therefore amount to termination of the contract. It would appear that an employee is under no obligation to accept wages in lieu of notice, and an employee who seeks re-instatement rather than compensation may be advised in the circumstances to refuse the payment.

Frustration

A contract is frustrated if its performance in its original form becomes impossible, due to a supervening event producing a situation radically different from that envisaged by the parties when they entered into the contract.

The most common events in the present employment field are concerned with the illness and imprisonment of employees. However, these are not the only circumstances in which a contract is frustrated. In *Morgan v. Manser*, a music hall artiste entered into a ten-year agreement to offer his services solely to his manager, in return for an undertaking to secure engagements. Manser served in the armed services during the Second World War and later entered into engagements with other agents. It was held that the period of military service had frustrated the contract.

Illness

The illness or incapacity of an employee may be of such a nature as to lead to the frustration of a contract. In *Condor v. Barron Knights*, a young drummer was unable to fulfill a five-year contract with a pop group and play on seven nights a week. On medical advice he was only allowed to play on four nights a week. As there was no likelihood of his being able to resume normal employment in the near future the contract was held to be frustrated.

If there is a likelihood of the employee recovering and substantially performing his contract it will not be regarded as frustrated. In *Storey v. Fulham Steel Works*, a works manager was engaged on a five-year agreement, with no provision as to notice. After two years employment he became ill and was absent from time to time. The employer purported to terminate the agreement but was informed by the employee that he had recovered from illness and would shortly be returning to work. It was held that his illness under this agreement was not of such a character as to indicate that he would never be able to perform his contract and that he would have to be reinstated immediately.

The risk of illness of an employee cannot be a ground for frustration of a contract, unless the nature of the employment was such that it would be unsafe for the employee to continue in that employment. In *Converfoam (Darwen) v. Bell*, a works director who had a heart attack returned to work to be offered an alternative post at a lower salary. He refused and was dismissed. The employers contended that as there was a risk of the employee suffering further heart attacks, the contract was frustrated. It was held that as the employee was fit to resume normal employment, the possibility of an unforeseen risk did not frustrate the contract and he was held to be unfairly dismissed.

Employers have attempted to use the doctrine in situations where an employee has been ill and off work for some time and has not shown any signs of imminent recovery. The Employment Appeal Tribunal, in *Harman v. Flexible Lamps Ltd*, declared that 'in the employment field the concept of discharge by operation of law, that is frustration, is normally only in play where the contract of employment is for a long term which cannot be determined by notice. Where the contract is terminable by notice, there is really no need to consider the question of frustration and if it were the law that an employer was in a position to say "this contract has been frustrated", then that would be a very convenient way in which to avoid the provisions of the Employment Protection (Consolidation) Act'.

An employer who seeks to terminate an employee's contract on the grounds of ill health must therefore be prepared, with few exceptions, to justify the dismissal as reasonable in the circumstances.

In *Marshall v. Harland and Wolff Ltd*, Sir John Donaldson laid down the following guidelines which should be considered when deciding whether a contract was frustrated:

1   The terms of the contract, including any provisions for sick pay;
2   How long the employment was likely to last in the absence of sickness (temporary employment, or employment for the duration of a specific job, is more likely to be terminated than long-term employment);
3   The nature of the employment (the contract of an employee holding a key post, which must be filled on a permanent basis if his absence is prolonged, is more likely to be frustrated than that of an employee whose post could be kept open for a considerable time);
4   The nature of the illness, how long it has continued, and the prospects of recovery;
5   The period of past employment (a long-standing relationship is more likely to survive than one of short standing).

A contract may nevertheless be frustrated even though it is of a short duration. Most such cases have involved contracts of theatrical artistes. In *Poussard v. Spiers*, an opera singer was taken ill and failed to attend rehearsals or the first four performances of the opera. The replacement singer would only agree to appear if she were offered the complete engagement. It was held that the contract was frustrated. A contract will not be frustrated where the breach consists of a breach of warranty only. In *Bettini v. Gye*, a singer's failure to appear at rehearsals was regarded as a minor breach of the whole contract, i.e. a breach of warranty. The contract was not frustrated, as she was able and willing to appear at the theatre for the opera performances.

Imprisonment

The contract of an employee sentenced to a term of imprisonment may well be automatically terminated by frustration. In *Harrington v. Kent County Council*, the contract of a teacher sentenced to twelve months' imprisonment was held to be terminated by frustration. The employer was entitled to judge the contractual position at the time when the sentence was imposed. It was immaterial that the employer was aware of the employee's appeal against sentence, as the conviction and sentence of imprisonment were events which has frustrated the contract.

In *Chakki v. United Yeast Co. Ltd*, an employee was sentenced to eleven months imprisonment at the commencement of his two weeks' annual holiday. His employers immediately arranged a replacement. After spending one night in prison he was released on bail, and on appeal his sentence was varied to a term of probation. It was held that the contract was not frustrated. The EAT stated that the following questions must be considered when deciding whether a contract of employment has been frustrated by a prison sentence.

1 Is it commercially necessary to decide the employee's future and is a replacement necessary?
2 What is the likely length of the employee's absence?
3 If it is necessary to employ a replacement, is it reasonable to employ a permanent replacement rather than a temporary one?

Employees of partnerships and companies

Partnerships
Although a partnership is dissolved on the death or retirement of a partner, the death of a partner will not automatically terminate a contract of employment of a partnership employee, unless the contract is dependent on that partner's continued existence. Such a termination amounts to a dismissal for the purposes of redundancy (EPCA, section 93.1). However, the retirement of a partner and the subsequent transfer of the business to the remaining partners automatically terminates the contract of a partnership employee, unless there is a stipulation to the contrary in his contract. In these circumstances an employee should mitigate his loss if possible, so that if he is offered employment by the remaining partners on similar terms to his previous employment and refuses, he will only be entitled to nominal damages at common law for breach of contract. This rule must now be viewed in the light of the Transfer of Undertakings (Protection of Employment) Regulations 1981 which provide that where one person transfers a business in the nature of a commercial venture to another the transfer shall not operate so as to

terminate a contract of employment. An employee of a partnership whose business is taken over by a new partnership would therefore, under these regulations, be unable to claim damages for wrongful dismissal. It would however be regarded as constituting a dismissal for redundancy purposes.

An employee who is offered and who accepts employment in a reconstituted partnership (containing some of the old partners) will preserve his continuity of employment, as will an employee of a business which changes hands. The Transfer of Undertakings (Protection of Employment) Regulations provide that on the transfer of a commercial undertaking, e.g. the sale of a partnership, an employee who was employed by the old employer at the time of the transfer will automatically become an employee of the new employer, as if his contract of employment had originally been made with the new employer.

Companies

The appointment of a receiver by the court automatically terminates the contracts of a company's employees, but in other circumstances such an appointment does not of itself constitute a dismissal of the company's employees. A receiver is usually appointed by a creditor, e.g. a bank, when a company defaults on the repayment of interest or principal on a loan secured on the company's undertaking. If the receiver sells the undertaking, or his appointment is inconsistent with the continuance of an employee's contract (e.g. that of the managing director) this will constitute a dismissal.

The compulsory winding-up of a company operates as a notice of dismissal to its employees. The effect of a voluntary winding-up is not so drastic – a company's employees are only dismissed if the company is insolvent and therefore unable to fulfill its obligations under the contract.

Wrongful dismissal

If an employer does not give proper notice to an employee, he may be sued for wrongful dismissal. It is a breach of contract for either party to terminate a contract of employment without giving proper notice. The summary dismissal of an employee may only be justified by showing that the employer had sufficient grounds for taking such action. The numerous examples of such dismissals from the last century and from the early part of this century provide an unreliable guide to present day tests and changing social conditions.

The breach of a major term of a contract of employment usually provides justification for the dismissal of an employee without notice, e.g. theft from the employer, accepting bribes, incompetence, and immorality. All the circumstances surrounding the dismissal must be examined to determine whether a right of summary dismissal exists. The misconduct of an employee during working hours is far more likely to justify summary dismissal than any misconduct outside working hours.

An employer who is sued for wrongful dismissal may justify the dismissal on grounds which were not known to him at the time of the dismissal but which subsequently come to light (*Boston Deep Sea Fishing Company v. Ansell.*)

An employee who is not given the proper period of notice, or whose summary dismissal is not justified, may refuse to accept an employer's repudiation of the contract, as repudiation by one party does not of itself discharge the contract. The contract of employment is only discharged when the repudiation is accepted by the other party. However, the acceptance of new employment and/or claim for damages by an employee implies acceptance of the repudiation.

A fixed-term contract, i.e. a contract made for a specified period of time, will terminate on the expiration of that time. In this situation an employee cannot claim that he has been wrongfully dismissed, but he is entitled to bring an action for unfair dismissal if the contract is not renewed (see page 107).

A contract of employment will be terminated by the death of either party. There is an obligation to pay any wages which have accrued. Special provisions are found in schedule 12 of the EPCA which govern any entitlement to a redundancy payment and compensation for unfair dismissal on the death of either party, after an employee's dismissal.

An employee who is dismissed almost invariably brings an action for unfair dismissal (see Chapter 8), rather than suing in the courts for wrongful dismissal. An action for unfair dismissal is heard by an industrial tribunal which offers a speedier, cheaper and less formal means of providing redress for a dismissed employee. It also offers alternative remedies to those provided by the courts, i.e. compensation as well as the possibility of re-instatement or re-engagement.

However, there are certain circumstances when a dismissed employee will bring an action for wrongful dismissal.

1 When he is not entitled to bring an action for unfair dismissal as he comes within the excluded categories, or he has less than fifty-two weeks' continuous employment (see page 103).

2 If he is a highly-paid employee (e.g. a managing director of a company) who is engaged on a fixed term contract or entitled to a lengthy period of notice, and has been wrongfully and unfairly dismissed. Such an employee would seek damages for wrongful dismissal in preference to a claim for compensation for unfair dismissal, which is subject to statutory limits (see page 125).

Remedies following termination of the contract

1 *Declaration* An employee may seek a declaration from the court that he was wrongfully dismissed and that he is still employed.

2 *Damages* An employee may sue an employer where the employer is in breach of his contractual duties.

3 *Specific performance* A court order compelling the performance of an act.

4 *Injunction* An employer may seek an injunction, i.e. an order of the court which forbids the performance of a particular act or course of action.

1 Declaration

An employee may seek a declaration that his dismissal was wrongful and invalid. The court is asked to declare the position in law on a given set of facts. The declaration has coercive effect in that its terms are generally observed by the affected parties. A declaration will not generally be granted to an ordinary employee who is wrongfully dismissed, except in special circumstances.

Employees who enjoy a special statutory status may seek a declaration. In *Vine v. National Dock Harbour Board*, a registered dock worker obtained a declaration that his purported dismissal by a disciplinary board was null and void, as his name had not been validly removed from the register. He remained in the employment of the National Dock Harbour Board.

A chief constable was granted a declaration that his dismissal was null and void, and was consequently able to safeguard his pension rights (*Ridge v. Baldwin*).

The courts will more readily grant a declaration when the facts in issue raise the problem of a right to work rather then the right to remain with a particular employer. In *Nagle v. Fielden*, the Jockey Club refused Mrs Nagle a licence to train racehorses in pursuance of their unwritten policy of not granting a licence to a woman. She obtained a declaration that the practice was contrary to public policy. The parties later reached a settlement and she was granted a trainer's licence.

In *Bonsor v. Musicians Union*, a professional musician was granted a declaration that his expulsion from the Musicians Union was null and void. The branch secretary had removed his name from the register without consulting the branch committee, as was required by the union rules.

2 Damages

An employee who is wrongfully dismissed may sue his employer for damages. The basis of compensation is twofold.

Firstly, the employee should be placed in the same financial position as if the contract had not been broken, i.e. he should be given the wages he would have received had proper notice been given to him on the date of dismissal. An employee on a fixed-term contract will be able to recover as damages the salary or wages payable for the balance of the unexpired term.

Secondly, he should receive such damages as may reasonably supposed to have been in the contemplation of the parties, at the time of making the contract, as the probable result of the breach (*Clayton v. Oliver*).

An employee will therefore be able to recover the amount of wages that he would have received, but for his wrongful dismissal. He will of course be entitled to any unpaid wages at the date of his dismissal. He will also be entitled to compensation for any loss of fringe benefits, e.g. the use of a car, accrued pension rights.

The purpose of an award of damages is to compensate an

employee for any loss sustained as a result of a breach of contract. If an employee obtains other employment before the expiration of the term of the breached contract, earnings from the new employment will be deducted from the damages.

An employee is under a duty to mitigate the loss if possible, by obtaining new or alternative employment. In *Brace v. Calder*, an employee, dismissed on the dissolution of a partnership, refused similar employment offered to him by the new partnership which took over from the 'old' firm. He was awarded nominal damages, as he should have accepted this offer of new employment and minimised his loss.

A court in assessing damages may well take into account various benefits paid to the employee, e.g. unemployment benefit, or supplementary benefit. These have been taken into account when assessing damages in personal injury cases. Whether a redundancy payment may be deducted from the assessed damages is questionable and depends on the circumstances surrounding the employee's dismissal.

An employee's liability to taxation must also be taken into account when awarding damages, as the employee's wages would have been subject to income tax if he had continued in that employment (*Beech v. Reed Corrugated Cases Ltd*).

An employee is not entitled to claim damages for the manner of his dismissal, for his injured feelings, or for any loss he may suffer from the fact that the dismissal makes it more difficult to obtain new employment. In *Addis v. Gramaphone Company*, the plaintiff was employed as the manager at its Calcutta office. He was given six months' notice by his employer and was prevented from acting any longer as manager. He was entitled to damages for loss of six months' salary and commission, but there was no entitlement for the way in which the dismissal had been carried out.

However, in *Cox v. Phillips Industries*, it was held that damages may be awarded if the employer's conduct on terminating the contract is such that it causes mental distress to the employee. In this case the plaintiff was relegated to a less responsible position as a result of submitting a letter asking for a review of his salary. Although his salary was unaffected, his new duties were extremely vague, and he became very depressed, anxious and frustrated. Following pressure from the company he was induced to sign a letter of resignation. It was held that the company was in breach of contract by relegating the employee to a less responsible position and by subjecting him to mental distress.

An action for wrongful dismissal must be commenced within a period of six years from the date of the breach of the contract. A claim for £500 or less is heard by the Registrar in the County Court. If the sum claimed exceeds £500, but is less than £5000, the case is heard in the County Court. All claims in excess of £5000 must be commenced in the High Court.

3 Specific performance

A decree of specific performance will not be granted by a court or tribunal to compel an employee to continue to work for a particular employer. Section 16 of TULRA provides that 'no court shall, whether by way of (*a*) an order for specific performance . . . of a contract of employment, or (*b*) an injunction . . . restraining a breach or threatened breach of such a contract, compel an employee to do any work or attend at any place for the doing of any work'.

However, the EPCA provides a remedy, which bears a close resemblance to specific performance. If an industrial tribunal finds that an employee has been unfairly dismissed it may ask the employee if he wishes the tribunal to make an order for re-instatement or re-engagement. Re-instatement is a restoration of the employee to his former post, while an order for re-engagement requires an employer to find comparable or other suitable work for the employee.

4 Injunction

An injunction (a court order prohibiting the recipient from carrying out an act) is sometimes sought by an employer who seeks to protect certain legitimate business interests. He may allege than en employee is in breach of a restrictive employment covenant or has failed to show good faith towards his employer.

In *Thomas Marshall (Exporters) v. Guinle*, a managing director repudiated a ten-year service agreement with the company and resigned. He then solicited business from the company's customers in breach of his service agreement. The company was granted an injunction to enforce the covenant and prevent the defendant from avoiding his obligations under the contract.

A court will not grant an injunction where damages provide an adequate remedy, or if it compels the performance of a contract of employment. An injunction may be granted to enforce a negative stipulation in a contract, where damages fail to provide an adequate remedy. In *Lumley v. Wagner*, an opera singer, Joanna Wagner contracted to sing at Lumley's theatre for a period of three months, and covenanted that she would not sing elsewhere during that time without his written consent. An injunction was granted to restrain her from singing for another party in breach of the agreement, although a decree of specific performance was refused.

The granting of an injunction may have the effect of encouraging an employee to fulfill a contract of employment. In *Warner Bros v. Nelson*, the actress Bette Davis entered into a contract to devote her services exclusively to the film company for a certain length of time. During this time she also entered into a contract with an English film company. The court granted an injunction to Warner Bros, as her contract contained a negative stipulation that she would not work for another person during this time. As the injunction was confined to work on stage and screen she would be able to earn her living in another capacity and would not (in theory) be compelled to work for Warner Bros.

In *Page One Records Ltd v. Britton,* a pop group 'The Troggs' dispensed with the services of the company, who acted as their manager, in breach of a five-year contract. The company sought an injunction to prevent the group from appointing a manager until an action for breach of contract was heard by the court. This was refused, as it would compel the group to employ the company. The contract was for personal services of a fiduciary nature which could not be continued when one of the parties had lost confidence in the other.

It remains to be seen what effect section 16 of TULRA will have on the granting of injunctions in respect of contracts of employment, as the provisions of the Act would appear to limit the discretion of the judiciary in this particular area.

8

Unfair Dismissal

An action for unfair dismissal will be heard by an industrial tribunal which will enquire into the overall merits of the dismissal. Every dismissal, with or without notice, is presumed to be unfair and it is for the employer to justify the dismissal. At common law an employer may dismiss an employee for any reason as long as he gives the appropriate period of notice, or pays wages or salary in lieu of notice and in these circumstances an employee has no redress whatsoever in the courts.

In order to bring an action for unfair dismissal an employee must have the appropriate period of continuous employment and must not come within the limited categories of employees who are excluded from the unfair dismissal provisions (see page 103).

Continuity of employment

An employee must have been continuously employed for certain minimum periods of time before he can qualify for most statutory employment rights, e.g. two years for maternity pay or a redundancy payment, one year before he can bring an action for unfair dismissal.

The minimum periods of notice required to be given by an employer to terminate a contract of employment will vary according to the length of continuous employment of an employee, as follows:

(a) One week if employed for more than one month but for less than two years.

(*b*)   Not less than one week for each year, if employed for two years or more, but less than twelve years.

(*c*)   Not less than three months if employed for twelve years or more.

An employee must give at least one week's notice if he has been employed for more than one month. Any week in which an employee is employed for sixteen hours or more will count as a week in computing a period of employment. If an employee's working week changes from sixteen hours or more, to more than eight hours, but less than sixteen hours per week, he is entitled to count up to twenty-six weeks of this reduced working week towards continuity of employment. An employee who has worked for more than eight hours, but less than sixteen hours a week, for five years or longer, is deemed to have been continuously employed for the purposes of entitlement to these statutory rights.

Continuity is preserved even when an employee is on strike. The period of time on strike, however, does not count towards the total period of employment. The continuity of an employee who is dismissed during a strike and subsequently re-engaged is preserved, although again the period of time on strike does not count towards the total period of employment.

Continuity is also preserved in the following circumstances, even though there is a temporary break in employment:

1   If an employee whose contract has been terminated because of sickness or injury is re-engaged under a new contract, and this happens not more than twenty-six weeks after the end of the previous contract.

2   If there is a temporary cessation of work of the kind the employee was previously contracted to do. It was held in 1983 by the House of Lords in *Ford v. Warwickshire County Council* that a schoolteacher who had been employed for eight years under a series of contracts commencing each year in September and terminating in July had been continuously employed during that time. The summer holidays were regarded as a temporary cessation of work as the period of absence was short in relation to the length of the actual employment.

3   In circumstances in which, by arrangement or custom, the

employment is regarded as continuing, e.g. an employee is loaned to another employer.

4 When absence is due to pregnancy or confinement, as long as the employee returns to work with the employer or associated employer within twenty-nine weeks from the confinement.

5 In the four weeks which are permitted before re-engagement under a different contract of employment.

The periods of employment to be taken into account are those with the present employer. There are, however, certain circumstances where a change of employer does not break an employee's continuity of employment. They include:

1 The transfer of a trade or business to another employer;

2 The employees of a deceased employer being offered employment on similar terms by his personal representatives;

3 A change in the partners, trustees or personal representatives who are the employers;

4 Employment by an associated company i.e. a subsidiary or a holding company or a company controlled by the same person;

5 A relevant transfer within the meaning of the Transfer of Undertakings (Protection of Employment) Regulations 1981. When a business is sold or disposed of (other than by a share take-over) the employees of the old employer will automatically become employees of the new employer, as if their contracts of employment were originally made with the new employer.

Excluded categories

Certain categories of employees are excluded from the unfair dismissal provisions. These are:

1 An employee with less than fifty-two weeks' continuous employment;

2 An employee who has been continuously employed for less than two years with a firm employing twenty employees or less;

3 An employee who before the effective date of termination of his/her employment had reached the normal retiring age of his/her employment or, if there is no normal retiring age, had

reached pensionable age i.e. sixty-five for men, sixty for women;

4 An employee who under his contract of employment ordinarily works outside Great Britain;
5 A registered dock worker engaged on dock work;
6 The master or member of crew of a fishing vessel who is paid solely by a share in the profits or gross earnings of the vessel;
7 A member of the armed forces or the police force;
8 A person employed under a fixed-term contract for two years or more, which was entered into before 28 February 1972;
9 A person employed under a fixed-term contract for one year or more who, before the expiry of the contract, has agreed in writing to waive the right of complaint of unfair dismissal on the contract's expiry;
10 A person covered by a dismissal procedures' agreement, entered into after 1 October 1980, which has been exempted from the unfair dismissal provisions by an order made by the Secretary of State for Employment;
11 A person who did not present a complaint of unfair dismissal within three months of the effective date of termination or within such further time as is considered reasonable;
12 A person who is involved in industrial action at the date of the dismissal.

A claim from a person falling within of the first three categories will not be excluded if the reason for the dismissal was the employee's membership of a trade union, his trade union activities, or his refusal to join a trade union or to remain a member of a trade union.

Dismissal

An employee is treated as dismissed by his employer if:

1 The employer terminates the contract, with or without notice; or
2 The employee terminates the contract, with or without notice, by reason of the employer's conduct (constructive dismissal); or
3 A fixed term contract expires and is not renewed.

1 Termination by employer

In the majority of cases an employee will be given proper notice by his employer in accordance with the terms of the contract. If notice is not given the intention of the parties must be ascertained. If an employee is told to 'collect your cards' or 'you're fired', the intention is quite clear, but in other cases words spoken in the heat of the moment may well be viewed in a different light at a later time by the parties.

If an employee is given a choice of resignation or dismissal, this Hobson's choice will constitute a dismissal. In *Robertson v. Securicor Transport Ltd*, an employee was in breach of a company rule when he signed for a container which he had not received. When this was discovered he was given the option of resigning or being dismissed. Although he resigned, he was nevertheless held to have been dismissed.

If an employee who has been given notice by his employer, gives notice to his employer to terminate his employment on an earlier date than that specified in the employer's notice, he will nevertheless be taken as having been dismissed by the employer for the reasons given by the employer.

If an employee gives notice to his employer to terminate the contract of employment and the employer dismisses him (with or without notice) during the period of notice, this will constitute a dismissal rather than a resignation. In *Harris and Russel Limited v. Slingsby*, an employer ordered off the premises an employee who had given in his notice, when he discovered that the employee intended to work for a rival company. This was held to constitute a dismissal.

2 Constructive dismissal

An employee who does not give proper notice to his employer may justify his action on the grounds of 'constructive dismissal', i.e. the employer's conduct was such that he was entitled to terminate the contract without notice. Alternatively an employee may give notice and work the period of notice. In both situations the employer's breach of contract must be fundamental and significant, thereby justifying summary termination by the employee.

In *Western Excavating Ltd v. Sharp*, Lord Denning MR stated: 'If the employer is guilty of conduct which is a significant breach going to the root of the contract of employment, or which shows that the employer no longer intends to be bound by one or more of the essential terms of the contract, then the employee is entitled to treat himself as discharged from any further performance. If he does so, then he terminates the contract by reason of the employer's conduct. He is constructively dismissed. The employee is entitled in those circumstances to leave at the instant without giving any notice at all or, alternatively, he may give notice and say he is leaving at the end of the notice. But the conduct must in either case be sufficiently serious to entitle him to leave at once. Moreover, he must make up his mind soon after the conduct of which he complains; for, if he continues for any length of time without leaving, he will lose his right to treat himself as discharged. He will be regarded as having elected to affirm the contract'.

An employee must also show that the contract had not been terminated by the time the breach occurred, and the breach was the reason for its termination. An employee who continues to work after such a breach may well be regarded as affirming the contract and condoning the breach. If an employee is such a situation clearly objects, the fact that he continues to draw his wages does not necessarily indicate affirmation of the contract and acceptance of the breach.

Examples of constructive dismissals

In *Courtaulds Northern Textiles v. Andrew*, an overseer resigned after eighteen years' service, after an argument with an assistant manager when he was told that he could not 'do the bloody job anyway'. It was held that he was entitled to treat the comment as conduct justifying resignation, as it seriously damaged the relationship of confidence and trust between the parties.

In *Post Office v. Roberts*, an employee who had been appraised as capable asked for a transfer to a new area as she was getting married. She was told there were no suitable vacancies, but later discovered that a senior officer had written a poor assessment of her capabilities containing criticisms of which she had not been informed. She resigned and claimed a constructive dismissal. It was held that the Post Office's conduct was in breach of its implied obligation of mutual trust and confidence, which amounted to a repudiation of the contract.

In *Stokes v. Hampstead Wine Co.*, the employer agreed to pay overtime for Christmas work and an employee worked eighty-eight hours overtime over the Christmas period. Despite various promises she was not paid for those hours until the following February when she was paid for forty hours and was told that this was all she was getting. She informed the employers that she would resign if she did not receive the arrears by the following day. She was not paid, and so she resigned. It was held that this was a constructive dismissal as the employer was in fundamental breach of contract and the employee had acted reasonably.

In *Savoia v. Chiltern Herb Farms*, a company required the employee to change jobs as a result of reorganisation. He was previously supervisor of a packing department and was required to become production foreman. He refused on the ground that he would be exposed to conjunctivitis as a result of heat and smoke, but refused to submit to a medical examination, or provide evidence from his own doctor. It was held that he had been constructively, but fairly, dismissed.

An employee should not regard a statement by his employer that his employment will cease in the near future, and advising the employee to seek alternative employment, as a constructive dismissal. In *Heseltine Lake v. Dowler*, an employee was told that he no longer had a future with the firm and would be wise to seek other employment or face eventual dismissal. In *International Computers Limited v. Kennedy*, an employee was informed that the factory where she was employed was to be closed down within the next year and she should seek alternative employment as soon as possible.

Both Dowler and Kennedy failed in their respective actions for constructive dismissal, as in neither case was there a dismissal, and there was no evidence that the employers would not have given proper periods of notice.

3 Fixed-term contracts

An employee whose fixed-term contract is not renewed is regarded as having been dismissed. A fixed-term contract which may be terminated before the end of the fixed-term, by notice given by either party, is nevertheless regarded for the purposes of the EPCA as a contract for a fixed-term. An employee may forego his right to sue for unfair dismissal if a fixed-term contract is not renewed.

Reasons for dismissal

If it is established that a dismissal has taken place it must then be determined whether such a dismissal is fair. An employer who seeks to justify a dismissal must show that the reason (or principal reason) for dismissal was one of the following:

1 A reason related to the employee's capability or qualifications for performing the work in question;
2 A reason related to the employee's conduct;
3 That the employee was redundant;
4 That the employee could not continue to be employed in that capacity without contravening a statutory duty or restriction;
5 Some other substantial reason which would justify the dismissal of an employee holding the employee's position.

An employer must show that not only did he have a valid reason for the dismissal, but that he acted reasonably in the circumstances (including the size and administrative resources of the undertaking) in dismissing the employee for that particular reason. That question must be determined in accordance with equity and the substantial merits of the case.

The test of reasonableness involves a consideration of the steps leading up to a decision to dismiss the employee, together with a consideration of the way the dismissal was carried out. Previous warnings, hearings and appeals must all be considered to determine the reasonableness of the dismissal. If an employee is dismissed for lack of capability or misconduct, it is necessary to show that he was warned and given the opportunity to improve.

1 Capability and qualifications

Capability is assessed by reference to skill, aptitude, health or any other physical or mental quality; while qualifications refers to any degree, diploma or other academic, technical professional qualification relevant to the position which the employee held.

Capability

An employer may dismiss an employee who lacks the capability to perform the contract of employment in a satisfactory manner. Whether a dismissal is fair in these circumstances will depend on a variety of factors, e.g. the position held by the employee, the nature of the incompetence, whether an employee is given the opportunity to improve. The test is whether the employer honestly believes, on reasonable grounds, that the employee is incompetent.

In *Taylor v. Aidair Ltd*, it was held that a landing by airline pilot was so hazardous and incompetent as to justify instant and fair dismissal. In *Williams v. Mortimer Fashions Ltd*, it was held that an employee, the firm's financial director, was fairly dismissed as he had failed to keep the directors informed as to the company's financial situation, especially as to the extent to which overdue accounts had accumulated.

An employee whose work is criticised should be given an opportunity to improve. In *Tiptools v. Curtis*, an employee with over twenty years' satisfactory service was held to be unfairly dismissed when he was dismissed without warning for poor workmanship on an important order. In *Newalls Insulation Co. Ltd v. Blakeman*, an employee was held to be fairly dismissed after being absent on two occasions in a fortnight, following a final written warning for absenteeism.

In the case of a senior employee, one serious case of gross negligence may justify dismissal. In *Comerfood v. Swel Foods Ltd*, a factory supervisor was fairly dismissed when he allowed production to continue after realising that a pump was malfunctioning. The output of a whole shift had to be written off.

An employee who is promoted beyond his ability should, if possible, be offered alternative work as an alternative to dismissal. In *Coward v. John Menzies (Holdings) Ltd*, the manager of a branch was considered to be lacking in certain qualities. The employers decided that he needed re-training and proposed that he should be demoted to assistant manager and transferred to a branch two hundred miles away, but receive the same salary. Company policy was to re-train employees in this situation, and later re-promote if the re-training was successful. The employee declined the transfer and was dismissed. It was held that the dismissal was fair.

Ill health   A very important aspect of capability is the question of an employee's health. A dismissal of an employee on the grounds of ill health will be judged on the individual's circumstances as well as the nature and size of the organisation.

An employer must make a reasonable effort to establish the true medical position relating to the employee. In *East Lindsay District Council v. Daubney*, an employee who had suffered a stroke was held to be unfairly dismissed as a result of a medical report which merely stated that he should be retired early, but gave no medical details. The report had been obtained without the knowledge or consent of the employee, and there had been no proper investigation of the facts.

An employer acts reasonably if he relies on advice given by his own doctor, even if that advice conflicts with that given by the employee's own doctor. An employer should if possible seek alternative work for an employee who has become unfit to follow his present job. In *Carricks (Caterers) v. Nolan*, the dismissal of a maintenance fitter who had been off work with heart trouble was held to be unfair when he refused to work shifts. The employer could easily have re-organised matters to avoid Nolan lifting heavy weights, or arranged to offer him a day job.

Absence from work   The effect of an employee's absence on an employer's business has to be considered on a realistic basis. In *Spencer v. Paragon Wallpapers*, a small firm's only van driver was a fairly dismissed for repeated days absences. If a firm is able to find a temporary replacement it will be difficult for the employer to justify a dismissal.

It was stated in the above case that the factors which should be considered were: 'The nature of the illness; the likely length of the continuing absence, the need of the employers to have done the work which the employee was engaged to do'.

If an employee's absence affects the other employees, e.g. in performance or pay, or his absence is seriously damaging the firm's business, his dismissal may be regarded as fair. In *Tan v. Berry Brothers & Rudd Ltd*, an employee with a record of absenteeism required an operation. His subsequent dismissal was held to be fair as the employers, a small firm, were approaching the Christmas rush, and the continued absence of a single employee was significant in these circumstances.

Although a firm cannot wait indefinitely for the employee's return to work, the likelihood of an employee returning to work in the near future should be taken into account. In *Hawick v. Leeds Area Health Authority* a nurse was absent due to ill health for four months, her period of entitlement to sick pay under the Authority's scheme. She indicated that she would be returning to work in eight days' time. Her dismissal by the Authority on the termination of the period of entitlement was held to be unfair.

Absenteeism and late arrival at work are forms of misconduct which may, in certain circumstances, justify dismissal. The reason for the absence or lateness and the employee's work and attendance record must be taken into consideration in deciding whether there are grounds for dismissal. This situation usually requires that a warning be given, followed by a reasonable opportunity to improve.

In *London Transport Executive v. Clarke*, an employee was dismissed in 1979 because of his unauthorised absence in Jamaica for a period of seven weeks. He had visited the island in 1977, and the employer had a rule that unpaid leave for overseas visits would only be granted at intervals of three years or longer. This was held to be a fair dismissal, as he had been told that he would be dismissed if he went without permission.

Qualifications   There have been very few cases where the lack of qualifications have been the reason for the dismissal. In *Blackman v. Post Office*, a post and telegraph officer was required to pass an aptitude test within a specified time. He attempted the test on the permitted number of occasions but failed to pass. It was held that his dismissal related to a 'qualification'.

2   Conduct

The ACAS Code of Practice gives practical advice to employers on how to deal with disciplinary matters in a fair manner. Although the Code is advisory, a tribunal must consider any provisions of the Code which appear to be relevant in the matter before it. It must also decide to what extent it is necessary and practicable for an employer to follow the provisions of the Code. A tribunal must take into account the size and administrative resources of a business in determining whether an employer acted reasonably.

On joining a firm an employee should be given clear instructions as to the scope of his duties. He should be informed as to what conduct can lead to a dismissal, and in particular those offences which justify summary dismissal for a first offence.

The Code envisages the following stages:

(*a*)   An individual receiving a formal oral warning, or if the issue is more serious a written warning, setting out the nature of the offence and the likely consequences of further offences.

(*b*)   A final written warning, accompanied by a statement that any recurrence will lead to suspension or dismissal or some other penalty.

(*c*)   Disciplinary transfer or suspension (without pay if provided for in the contract), or dismissal according to the gravity of the offence.

Where appropriate an employee should be accompanied by a trade union representative or a fellow employee at the disciplinary interview, and should be given an opportunity to state his case.

The Code requires that some form of appeals procedure be instituted whenever possible, and that an employee should be given the opportunity to appeal to a level of management not previously involved. The essential features of disciplinary procedures and their operation is to be found in the Code.

Criminal offences   An employee's dishonesty may justify dismissal. The majority of cases have dealt with theft – from an employer, a fellow employee or a customer. Any of these will usually be regarded as clear grounds for dismissal.

In *Parker v. Dunn Ltd,* an employee admitted to the police that he had stolen from his employer. He complained that his subsequent dismissal was unfair as he had not been given the opportunity to state his case to his employers. It was held that his dismissal was fair, as he had not protested his innocence to his employers and had not sought to implement the available grievance procedure.

Theft from a fellow employee is viewed in a similar light. In *Fowler v. Camell Laird*, an employee stole a car mirror from a fellow employee's car parked in the works car park. His dismissal was held to be fair.

Where there is a suspicion of dishonesty, an employer should carry out an investigation, and where possible give the employee an opportunity to explain. In *Tesco Limited v. Hill*, an employee was suspended after failing to ring certain items on her till. She was dismissed later the same day after the employer had investigated the matter in her absence. The dismissal was held to be unfair as the employee should have been given the opportunity to offer an explanation.

An employer may dismiss an employee if he genuinely believes, on reasonable grounds, in the employee's guilt. Such a dismissal will be fair even though an employee may later be acquitted of the offence, or the police decline to prosecute.

In *Harris and Shepherd v. Courage Ltd*, two employees were charged with theft from their employer. The employer followed the agreed stages of disciplinary procedure, but the employees did not participate because of the pending trial. The employees were dismissed, but were later acquitted at the Crown Court. Their dismissal was held to be fair, for if an employee chooses not to give an explanation, an employer may consider the evidence and decide whether a dismissal is justified.

Different considerations may apply to an employee who commits a criminal offence outside his employment. The factors to be considered are stated in the ACAS Code of Practice, paragraph 15 (c).

An employee with twenty years service was apprehended at another store for shoplifting. She signed a form admitting taking the goods without paying. Although she later gave an explanation to her employers which was consistent with her innocence, she was held to have been fairly dismissed (*Moore v. C & A Modes*).

A college lecturer in charge of 16–18 year olds, convicted of gross indecency with another man in a public lavatory, was held to have been fairly dismissed by his employers (*Gardiner v. Newport County Council*).

Disobedience　An employer may dismiss an employee for refusing to obey a reasonable order. What is a reasonable order depends on the type and terms of employment and the employee's position. (*Union of Construction, Allied Trades & Technicians v. Brain* see page 40).

In *Bloomfield v. Trust Houses Forte Ltd*, an employee called a union meeting at a time when his employer had informed him that it was inconvenient to guests and he would be dismissed if he contravened the order. The dismissal was held to be fair. A lesbian refused to remove a badge proclaiming 'Lesbians Ignite'. As she was an accounts clerk whose duties involved contact with the public, it was held that her subsequent dismissal was fair (*Boychuk v. H. J. Symons Holdings Ltd*).

An employee has a right to object if an order affects or alters terms of employment, the type of work undertaken, his pay, hours of work, or conditions of work. These must be balanced against the employer's needs. In *Johnson v. Nottinghamshire Police Authority*, an employee who refused to change from day working to day, evening and shift working was held to be fairly dismissed (see page 133).

It was stated by Watkins L. J. in *Woods v. W. M. Car Services,* 'Employers must not be put in a position where, through the wrongful refusal of their employees to accept change, they are prevented from introducing improved business methods in furtherance of seeking success for their enterprise'.

An employee who disobeys a disciplinary rule may find that his conduct justifies dismissal. In *Singh v. Lyons Maid Ltd*, an employee, a Sikh, was dismissed for contravening company hygiene rules by wearing a beard. He was engaged in the manufacture of ice-cream, and was told that unless he removed the beard he could not continue as a production worker. He refused to do so on religious grounds. His dismissal was held to be fair.

In *Kingston and Richmond Area Health Authority v. Kaur* a nurse who refused to comply with an order to wear a uniform and persisted in wearing trousers was held to have been fairly dismissed.

However, in *Elliott Brothers v. Colverd*, an employee who was summarily dismissed for clocking in a fellow worker was held to have been unfairly dismissed. The offence had never been specifically defined as one which would result in instant dismissal.

Whether swearing by an employee can justify dismissal depends on the employee's status, the circumstances, the location of the work, and who is in receipt of the employee's invective. An apprentice was dismissed when on being criticised by the managing director about a job, replied 'you couldn't have done any f....ng better'. It was held that the dismissal was unfair as it was an isolated incident. The employer was also, to some extent, *in loco parentis* to the employee. The apprentice was awarded two years pay as compensation (*Shortland v. Chantrill*).

In *Rosenthal v. Louis Butler Ltd* an employee was dismissed for calling the factory manager 'a great fat punk' (his version) or 'a stupid punk' (her version) in the presence of other employees. It was held that her dismissal was unfair. It was 'a small friendly factory in East London where . . . language can be robust at times'. There should have been a warning before dismissal was contemplated.

3 Redundancy

An employee who satisfies certain statutory requirements is entitled, in a redundancy situation, to receive a redundancy payment. This entitlement does not of itself make the dismissal fair, or constitute sufficient grounds for dismissal.

There are certain situations where a selection for redundancy is regarded as unfair (EPCA, section 59). The dismissal will be held to be unfair if an employee shows that the circumstances constituting the redundancy applied equally to one or more other employees, but they have not been dismissed by the employer, and the reason for selecting the employee was one of the following:

(*a*) The employer without special reason disregarded the customary arrangement or agreed procedure relating to the selection of employees for redundancy; or

(*b*) The employee was selected for redundancy on account of trade union membership or activities; or

(*c*) The employee was selected for redundancy as he did not belong to a trade union.

A comparison must be made with other employees holding similar positions. Tribunals have not relied on titles or gradings, but have looked at the work that is actually done, and its interchangeability with other work in the same undertaking. An undertaking may cover several establishments within a group or a company. In *Oxley v. Tarmac Roadstone Holdings*, two plants situated a quarter of a mile apart had the same works manager. Different hours were worked at the plants, which had different facilities. Nevertheless the plants were not regarded as separate entities.

A customary arrangement is an arrangement which is so well

known, clear and certain that it effectively amounts to an implied agreed procedure. It must therefore exist with a degree of notoriety among the work force. An employee cannot merely assert that 'last-in, first-out' is a general custom which is universally recognised. He must be able to show that this is a customary arrangement which exists in the undertaking in which he is employed.

An employee who complains that the employer did not follow the agreed procedure must show (*a*) that there was a procedure, (*b*) that he was selected for redundancy in breach of that procedure, and that (*c*) there were no special reasons justifying a departure from that procedure.

An employer must show that he acted reasonably in the circumstances. In *Williams v. Compar Maxam Ltd*, a union was informed that the company proposed to make twenty-one employees redundant: By agreement with the union volunteers were sought, but only seven employees volunteered. The employers then selected the remaining persons to be made redundant, without consulting the union, and dismissed them on the day after the union had been informed of the redundancies, but with no list of names. It was held that the dismissals were unfair. Not only must an employer show that it was reasonable to dismiss an employee, he must also show that it was reasonable to dismiss the employee concerned.

It was stated in *Williams v. Compair Maxam Ltd,* that where employees are represented by an independent union an employer should adopt the following principles:

1   To give as much warning as possible of impending redundancies;
2   To consult with the union as to the best means of achieving management's desired result fairly with the minimum hardship to employees;
3   To attempt to agree criteria to be applied in selecting employees for redundancy;
4   To consider together with the union, when a selection has been made, whether the criteria have been applied;
5   To establish criteria (in cases where no criteria have been agreed) which can be objectively checked against various factors, e.g. attendance record, efficiency, experience or length of service to try to ensure that selection is fair and accords with the criteria and to consider union representations;

6   To see whether alternative employment can be offered to the employee rather than dismissal.

An employer must therefore show that he acted reasonably in the circumstances. The following have been regarded as unreasonable conduct on the employer's part, rendering a dismissal unfair: unreasonable selection made between comparable employees; failure to adopt a proper procedure of warnings and consultation; and failure to seek alternative employment for an employee before declaring him redundant. An employer also has a duty to consult trade union representatives on impending redundancies.

If the dismissal is found to be unfair, it is possible for an employee to be awarded compensation for unfair dismissal, and a redundancy payment in respect of the same dismissal. The basic award will, however, be adjusted to take account of the redundancy payment.

4   Contravention of statute

An employee may be dismissed if his continued employment contravenes a duty or restriction imposed by the law, e.g. the failure of an employee to obtain a work permit.

In *Appleyard v. Smith (Hull) Ltd*, a mechanic lost his driving licence and he was dismissed. It was held that it was essential for him to test-drive vehicles, and as it was impossible for the firm to employ him in any other capacity until his licence was restored, his dismissal was fair.

In *Gill v. Walls Meat Co. Ltd*, a Sikh employee who dealt with raw meat, grew a beard in accordance with his faith (when he was initially employed he was clean shaven). As it would be an offence under the Food Regulations 1970 to continue to employ him in this capacity, he was offered alternative employment. He refused and his subsequent dismissal was held to be fair.

5   Some other substantial reason

If an employer dismisses an employee for some other substantial reason, he must show that the reason warranted dismissal and the dismissal was reasonable in the circumstances.

Section 61 of the EPCA provides for two circumstances which amount to a substantial reason. Both deal with the dismissal of a temporary replacement, who was engaged to replace a woman who is absent because of pregnancy or confinement, or engaged to replace an employee suspended on medical grounds. In both cases the replacement must have been informed in writing of the temporary nature of the employment and that he or she may be dismissed when the absent employee returns to work.

Other cases falling into this general residuary category have dealt with a variety of situations.

In *Priddle v. Dibble*, a farm labourer was dismissed and replaced by the employer's son. The son had farming experience and was competent to do mechanical work on the farm, which the labourer could not do. The employee knew when he was first employed that the son would eventually work on the farm. It was held to be a fair dismissal, as there was insufficient work for both men.

In *Storey v. Allied Brewery*, a company introduced a rota system of work which included Sunday working. An employee was held to have been fairly dismissed when she refused to work on Sundays, as she wished to attend church. The change in working was necessary in the interests of economy.

An employee was held to be fairly dismissed when he refused to accept a change in pay, as the employer had inadvertently breached government policy in calculating the employee's pay. He refused, even though the amount was a loss of seventy-three pence over a period of ten weeks. He left the employment and unsuccessfully complained of constructive dismissal (*Industrial Rubber v. Gillon*).

In *Moreton v. Selby Protective Clothing Co. Ltd*, an employee had a provision in her contract giving her time off for school holidays. She was dismissed when she refused to make alternative arrangements which would allow her to work during those holidays. It was held that the dismissal was fair, as the production difficulties encountered by the firm had priority over domestic arrangements.

Union membership and the closed shop

Union membership
A dismissal by an employer will be regarded as unfair if the reason, or principal reason was that an employee:

1 Was, or proposed to become, a member of an independent trade union

2 Was not a member of any trade union, or of a particular trade union and had refused to become or to remain a member
3 Had taken part, or proposed to take part, at any appropriate time in the activities of an independent trade union.

Appropriate time in this context is defined as outside working hours, or a time within working hours when, with the employer's consent, or by arrangement, it is permissible to take part in such activities. *Working hours* means any time when an employee is required to be at work in accordance with his contract of employment.

An employee dismissed for any of these reasons may bring a claim for unfair dismissal, however long his period of service, i.e. it is not necessary to have the normal qualifying period of one year (or two years where appropriate). He may also apply to an industrial tribunal for interim relief, i.e. relief pending the full hearing of the complaint for unfair dismissal. If the tribunal considers that the complaint will be upheld when the case is heard, it may order re-instatement or re-engagement, or make an order for the temporary continuation of the contract of employment.

A dismissal of an employee who is not a member of a specified trade union, or who refuses to join such a union in accordance with a union membership agreement (UMA), i.e. a closed shop, is fair as long as the closed shop has been approved in a secret ballot by eighty per cent of the employees covered by it, or by eighty-five per cent of those voting, in the preceding five years.

It is unfair to dismiss an employee in the following circumstances:

1 If an employee genuinely objects on the grounds of conscience or deeply held conviction to being a member of a trade union or of a particular union;

2 If an employee was employed in the class of employees covered by the closed shop agreement at the time of its introduction, and had not at any time been a member of a trade union in accordance with the agreement.

3 If in respect of a closed shop agreement taking effect after 14 August 1980, the agreement was not approved in a secret ballot by eighty per cent of the employees covered by it.

T.Y.E.L.—9

4   If at the time of the dismissal an employee has obtained or is seeking a declaration from an industrial tribunal that he has been unreasonably excluded or expelled from the trade union to which he has to belong, under the closed shop agreement.

5   If the employee is bound by his qualifications to observe a written code of conduct, and has either been expelled from his union, or refused to join a union, because of a conflict between that code and a union instruction to take industrial action.

An employee who cannot be fairly dismissed for not being a member of a trade union in a closed shop cannot be fairly dismissed for refusing to make payments to the trade union or to some other body or person in lieu of union membership.

Closed shop

A 'union membership agreement,' i.e. a closed shop, is an agreement:

(*a*)   Made by or on behalf of, or otherwise exists between, one or more employers and employer's associations;

(*b*)   Relating to employees of an identifiable class

(*c*)   With the effect in practice of requiring all the present employees of the class to which it relates to be or become a member of the union, or one of the unions which is or are parties to the agreement or arrangement, or of another specified independent trade union, whether or not there is a condition to that effect in their contract of employment.

A new Code of Practice on Closed Shop Agreements and Arrangements came into operation in 1983. It provides practical guidance on the making and operation of closed shop agreements, and can be taken into account by any court or industrial tribunal.

Pressure to dismiss unfairly

An employer who is forced to dismiss an employee as a result of the pressure of industrial action (calling, organising or procuring or financing a strike) or the threat of such pressure, may find that such a dismissal amounts to an unfair dismissal. No account must be taken of any pressure when deciding whether the employer had a sufficient reason for the dismissal or had acted reasonably.

If in proceedings before an industrial tribunal an employer claims that he was induced to dismiss an employee because of the pressure exercised on him, by a trade union or other person in calling, organising, procuring or financing a strike, or threatening to do so as the employee was not a member of a trade union or of a particular trade union, he may join that person as a party to the proceedings.

If a tribunal makes an award of compensation, but finds that the employer's claim is well founded, it may make an order requiring that person to pay the employer a contribution in respect of that compensation. The amount of the contribution shall be such as the tribunal considers to be just and equitable in the circumstances, and may constitute a complete indemnity.

Industrial action

An employee who is dismissed while participating in a strike or other industrial action, or in connection with a lock-out cannot claim that he was unfairly dismissed if: (*a*) the employer has dismissed all those who took part in the action at the same establishment as the complainant at the date of his dismissal, and (*b*) the employer has not offered re-engagement to any of them within three months of their date of dismissal, without making him a similar offer.

An employer may therefore dismiss all those employees who are on strike at the date of the dismissal. He is not to be regarded as acting unfairly by not dismissing employees who were on strike, but who had returned to work at the date of the dismissal. An employer may at any time after three months, re-engage a person dismissed for taking part in a strike. A person who is not offered re-engagement in these circumstances may not claim that he has been unfairly dismissed.

Pregnancy and confinement

An employee has the right not to be dismissed solely on the grounds that she is pregnant, or for any other reason connected with pregnancy (e.g. a miscarriage, post-natal illness), unless the employer can prove that (*a*) she was incapable of adequately doing her work because of her pregnancy, or (*b*) she could not carry on working without contravening a statutory provision relating to pregnant women. He must also prove that there was no suitable alternative vacancy which she could be offered, or if there was that she had been offered the vacancy, and refused it.

A woman has the right to return to work after her pregnancy or confinement. She can do so at any time before the end of the period of twenty-nine weeks, beginning with the week in which the date of confinement falls. She is entitled to return to her employment on terms and conditions which are no less favourable than those which would have been applicable had she not been absent. She must however give appropriate notice and satisfy the conditions for maternity pay listed on p. 84.

Failure to permit a woman to return to work after her pregnancy or confinement will not be treated as an unfair dismissal in the following circumstances:

(*a*)   Where immediately before her absence the number of employees employed by her employer and any associated employer totalled no more than five, and it was not reasonably practicable to re-instate her in her original job.

(*b*)   Where it was not reasonably practicable to re-instate her in her original job (for a reason other than redundancy), and she was offered alternative employment by her employer or an associated employer, which she accepted or unreasonably refused.

If there is no vacancy due to a redundancy situation, the employee may claim a redundancy payment and will be regarded as continuously employed until the notified date of her return to work. If, however, the employer can prove that the employee would have been made redundant on a particular day during her period of absence, her entitlement to a redundancy payment will be calculated up to that earlier day.

Remedies for unfair dismissal

The remedies available for unfair dismissal are:

1   Re-instatement;
2   Re-engagement;
3   An award of compensation.

An employee who complains of unfair dismissal must make an application on Form IT1 to an industrial tribunal.

A pertinent question on this form asks 'If the Tribunal decides that you were unfairly dismissed, please state which of the following you would prefer: re-instatement, re-engagement or compensation.'

1 Re-instatement

If a tribunal finds the complaint justified it must consider the possibility of re-instatement. This requires an employer to treat an employee in all respects as if he had not been dismissed. An employee is therefore entitled to any arrears of pay and to any benefits which have accrued during the period of his dismissal, e.g. if other employees on a similar grading and pay scale receive a pay increase during this time, the order will provide for the higher rate of pay from the date of its inception. All rights and privileges, including pension and seniority rights, must also be restored to the employee.

2 Re-engagement

Having decided that re-instatement is neither possible nor feasible, a tribunal may make an order for re-engagement. This is an order that the complainant be engaged by the employer, or his successor, or an associated employer, in employment which is comparable to his previous employment. Except in cases where an employee has contributed to his dismissal, the terms of the order should be, as far as reasonably practical, as favourable as an order for re-instatement. The order must also stipulate the future employer's identity, the nature of the employment, and the rate of pay.

In exercising its discretion for either of these remedies the tribunal must take into account the complainant's wishes, as an employee may not wish to be re-instated, and may prefer to return to his employment in a different job.

A tribunal must also consider whether re-instatement is a practical proposition for an employer. There may well have been a clash of personality between an employee and his fellow employees, or his supervisor, and this would continue if such an order was made.

A tribunal may not take into account the fact that an employer has engaged a permanent replacement for the dismissed employee, unless:

(a) The employer can prove that the employee's work could only be done by recruiting a permanent replacement; or

(b) A replacement was not appointed until a reasonable time had elapsed and the employer had not been informed by the dismissed employee that he wanted to be re-instated or re-engaged.

In calculating the amount of compensation payable for loss of benefits between the termination of the contract and re-instatement or re-engagement, a tribunal must take into account: wages in lieu of notice, ex gratia payments, payments from another employer during that period, and unemployment or supplementary benefits.

If a tribunal considers that an employee is partly to blame for his dismissal, it may make an order for re-instatement or re-engagement on less favourable terms, e.g. he should not receive full compensation for the loss of benefits.

A tribunal cannot have taken into account any matters of which an employer was unaware of at the time of the dismissal, as it has to consider the reason shown by the employer at the time of the dismissal. In *Davis & Sons v. Atkins*, an employee, the manager of an abattoir, refused to comply with his employers' wish that a considerable proportion of animals should be bought direct from farmers, rather than from dealers. He was dismissed, but was later offered an *ex gratia* severance payment. The employer later withdrew the offer on the grounds that they were treating his dismissal as a summary dismissal, on account of his gross misconduct during his term of employment, and which they were unaware of when he was dismissed. This was held to be an unfair dismissal.

3 Compensation

An award of compensation will be made:

(a) Where an employee indicates that he no longer wishes to return to work for his previous employers; or

(b) Where the tribunal decides that re-instatement or re-engagement is impracticable; or

(c) Where an employer fails to comply with an order for re-instatement or re-engagement.

Most employees who are successful in their claim for unfair dismissal are awarded compensation. The award will usually consist of a basic award and a compensatory award.

(i) Basic award
The basic award is calculated on a formula which is based on continuous employment, up to a maximum period of twenty years. An employee is entitled to the following amounts for each completed year of employment: one and a half weeks' pay for each year between the ages of forty-one and sixty-four (men); fifty-nine (women); one week's pay for each year between the ages of twenty-two and forty-one; half a week's pay for each year between the ages of eighteen and twenty-two.

The maximum amount of weekly pay which can be taken into account is currently £145. The maximum amount which is payable under this provision is therefore $20 \times 1\frac{1}{2} \times £145 = £4350$.

The basic award may be reduced if the employee:

(*a*) Unreasonably refused an offer of re-instatement;
(*b*) Had received a redundancy payment in respect of the same dismissal;
(*c*) Was within a year of his 65th (her 60th) birthday. The entitlement to the basic award must be reduced by one twelfth for every complete calendar month after the employee's 64th (or 59th) birthday.
(*d*) Had contributed to, or caused the dismissal, or his conduct prior to the dismissal justified the reduction.

(ii) Compensatory award
An employee may be awarded compensation for loss suffered as a result of his dismissal. The award is calculated on common law principles.

The various heads of compensation are as follows:

(a) Loss of earnings Loss of net earnings to the date of the hearing. This will include the period of notice if notice was not given. Deductions are not made for any sums earned during the period of notice, or for any supplementary or unemployment benefit received. A deduction will be made for any sickness benefit

received, if it is shown that had the employee remained in employment this amount would have been deducted from his wages.

(b) Manner of dismissal   Although an employee may not claim for any hurt feelings caused by the manner of his dismissal, he may nevertheless claim a sum if the manner of his dismissal could give rise to financial loss at a later date, e.g. by making the employee 'less acceptable to potential employers or exceptionally liable to selection for dismissal' (Sir John Donaldson in *Norton Tool Co. v. Tewson*).

(c) Estimated future loss of earnings   There must be evidence of probable future loss before this factor can be taken into consideration. The tribunal will make an assessment of the time it believes an employee is likely to be without employment, and will multiply the number of weeks of estimated unemployment by the employee's net wages. If an employee is likely to obtain employment, but at a lower wage, the tribunal will use the difference in net wages as a basis for its calculation. This is then multiplied by an estimate of the time it will take for the employee to obtain parity with his previous wages.

(d) Loss of statutory rights   An award may be made to compensate an employee for the loss of the periods of minimum statutory notice to which he is entitled. If an employee obtains new employment, it will take him fifty-two weeks to obtain protection against unfair dismissal with a new employer (a hundred and four weeks with an employer whose work force numbers twenty or less). After a period of four weeks employment, he will be entitled to one week's notice. An employee's entitlement to longer periods of notice is based on his years of continuous employment (see page 101). *In Daley v. Dorsett (Amar Dolls Ltd)*, it was suggested that an employee should receive compensation of half a week's net wages for the loss of every week of statutory notice. In this case the complainant, having worked for eight years, received an additional four weeks pay under this heading.

(e) Loss of pension rights   Any employee unfairly dismissed from pensionable employment, may claim under this heading. The burden of proving the loss and its extent lies on the dismissed employee. There are two distinct types of loss. Firstly, the loss of the pension position which has already been earned. Secondly, the loss of future

pension opportunity, i.e. the opportunity of improving this position until the time at which the pension becomes payable.

Two different methods of calculation are used:

(i) The employee and the employer's contributions to the date of dismissal are initially calculated. Compound interest from the date of payment is then assessed on these contributions. The grand total will then constitute the basis of the award.

(ii) A calculation of the capital sum required to purchase an annuity which is equal to the pension which he would ultimately receive.

The second calculation basis is appropriate for an employee who is close to retirement age.

Deductions

A tribunal must deduct a sum for an employee's contributory fault, for any redundancy payment received by the employee and for any failure of an employee to mitigate his loss. Sir John Donaldson, in *A. G. Bracey Ltd v. Iles*, stated: 'It may not be reasonable to take the first job that comes along. It may be much more reasonable, in the interests of the employee and the employer who has to pay compensation, that he should wait a little time. He must, of course, use the time well and seek a better paid job which will reduce his overall loss and the amount of compensation which the previous employer ultimately has to pay . . .'

In *Field v. Leslie & Goodwin Ltd*, an applicant, a placing broker, failed to register with agencies who might have been able to find him similar employment and also neglected to take up a good reference which had been promised. A tribunal assessed compensation on the basis that he would not have been out of work for more than four months if he had taken steps to mitigate his loss.

In *McGoldrick v. Robinson*, an employee was held to have failed to mitigate his loss when he refused the offer of his old job back, one week after being unfairly dismissed.

Failure to comply with an order

If an order is made for re-instatement or re-engagement and the terms of the order are not fully complied with, a tribunal must make an award of compensation, having regard to the loss sustained, up to a maximum of £7500.

If an employer fails to comply with a tribunal order for re-instatement or re-engagement the tribunal must make an additional award. The amount will depend on the reason for the original dismissal. The award will be for an amount equivalent to not less than thirteen weeks pay, but no more than twenty-six weeks pay. If the order for re-instatement or re-engagement relates to a dismissal which is in breach of the Race Relations Act or Sex Discrimination Act, the tribunal's award will be for an amount equivalent to not less than twenty-six weeks pay, but no more than fifty-two weeks pay.

If an employee requests re-instatement or re-engagement where the dismissal was for union membership or non-union membership, but the tribunal does not make such an order the award will be a week's pay multiplied by 104 or £10 000 whichever is the greater, up to a maximum of £20 000. If an employer fails to comply with an order for re-instatement or re-engagement for such a dismissal then, unless the employer is able to show that it was not practicable for him to comply, the award will be a week's pay multiplied by 156, or £15 000, whichever is the greater, with no maximum amount specified.

An employee may be awarded a further two weeks' pay if the employer fails to provide a written statement of reasons for his dismissal, when requested to do so by the employee.

The *maximum award* of compensation is payable to an employee with over twenty years service, after his forty-first birthday earning a minimum of £145 a week.

	£
Maximum basic award (£145 × 20 × 1½)	4350
Maximum compensatory award	7500
Maximum additional award of compensation	
(failure to re-engage or re-instate)	3770
(failure to re-engage or re-instate in	
race relations or sex discrimination case)	7540
	Total = 19 390

An additional two weeks' pay may be awarded for not providing written reasons for dismissal.

In cases involving dismissal for not joining a union, the maximum award could be:

	£
Maximum basic award	4350
Maximum compensation award	7500
Special award (156 × £145)	22 620
	Total = 34 470

Again, an additional two weeks' pay may be awarded for not providing written reasons for dismissal.

Dismissal procedure agreement

In certain circumstances the rights and procedures established under the EPCA in relation to unfair dismissal may be replaced by a dismissal procedure agreement. An application may be made jointly to the Secretary of State by all the parties concerned. The Secretary of State may make such an order if he is satisfied that:

(*a*)   Every trade union which is a party to the agreement is an independent trade union;

(*b*)   The agreement provides for procedures to be followed in cases where an employee claims that he has been unfairly dismissed;

(*c*)   Those procedures are available to all employees to which the agreement applies;

(*d*)   The remedies provided by the agreement in respect of unfair dismissal are on the whole as beneficial as those provided by the EPCA;

(*e*)   The procedures provided by the agreement include a right to arbitration or adjudication by an independent referee, tribunal, or other independent body in cases where there is a failure to reach a decision;

(*f*)   The provisions of the agreement are such that it can be determined with reasonable certainty whether the agreement applies to a particular employee.

9

Redundancy

The redundancy provisions of the EPCA provide for the payment of a lump sum to an employee who is dismissed due to redundancy, or who is laid off or kept on short time for a substantial period. The Act recognises the fact that an employee has an 'accrued right in his job' and provides a redundant employee with monetary compensation for its loss.

Redundancy provisions apply (with certain exceptions) to male employees under sixty-five and female employees under sixty who have been employed, after the age of eighteen, under a contract of employment, for at least two years. Certain workers are not included within the scope of the redundancy provisions, as they are not employees, or are covered by other arrangements, or their terms and conditions of employment are such that the application of the provisions would be inappropriate. These include fishermen, the majority of merchant seamen, Crown servants, National Health Service employees, employees who normally work outside the United Kingdom, domestic servants who are closely related to their employers, and self-employed individuals.

Dismissal for redundancy

When an employee claims, in proceedings before an industrial tribunal, an entitlement to redundancy compensation, it is presumed that his dismissal is for redundancy. This presumption may be rebutted by evidence given by the employer, by the employee or by the Department of Employment. The Department of Employment occasionally participates in redundancy proceedings, as it is an interested party in that if an employer makes a redundancy payment, the Department must grant him a rebate in respect of that payment.

A dismissal is due to redundancy if it is attributable wholly or mainly to the following facts:

1 The employer has ceased, or intends to cease, to carry on the business for the purposes for which the employee was employed by him;
2 the employer has ceased, or intends to cease, to carry on the business in the place where the employee was so employed;
3 the requirements of that business for employees to carry out work of a particular kind, or for employees to carry out work of a particular kind in the place where they were employed has ceased, or diminished, or is expected to cease or diminish.

1 The cessation of a business

The interpretation of this provision has caused relatively few problems, as the majority of dismissals under this provision are self-evident. It has been held that even a temporary cessation of business may amount to a redundancy situation. In *Gemmell v. Darngival Brickworks Ltd*, the applicant was held to be entitled to a redundancy payment when he was dismissed from the brickworks, which closed down temporarily for thirteen weeks for repairs to be made to machinery.

2 Change in the location of a business

An employee will not be justified in refusing to move to another location if his contract, or a collective agreement, or custom permits such a move. The majority of contracts of employment do not contain such provisions, and each case must be judged according to its merits. In *O'Brien v. Associated Fire Alarms*, the employee was an electrician employed to supply, install and maintain fire and burglar alarms in the Cheshire and Liverpool area. He was based at Liverpool and worked within a commutable distance from the city. The company proposed that he and fellow employees should work in Barrow in Furness, some 120 miles away. He refused and was dismissed. It was held that there was nothing in his contract to imply a term of mobility of that nature, and he was entitled to a redundancy payment.

A different conclusion was reached in *Stevenson v. Tees-side Bridge*, where a steel erector, who had worked at various times in different parts of the country, refused to work away from his home. It was held that his refusal was not justified, and that his subsequent dismissal was fair.

The removal of a business to a nearby location does not usually have the effect of constituting dismissal. A company which closed one of its restaurants in London offered its waitresses similar employment at another of its restaurants nearby. They refused, and it was held that their dismissal was fair (*Margiotta v. Mount Charlotte Investments Ltd*). Similarly in *Stevens v. Stitcher and Sons Ltd*, an employee who refused to transfer to a shop four hundred yards down the road was not entitled to a redundancy payment. However, in *Buck v. Edward Everard*, a Bristol printing company moved its premises to a suburb some seven miles away. It was held that Buck's refusal to move was justified, as mobility was not a factor which was normally encountered in the printing industry. He had been employed by the firm for a quarter of a century, and such a move would mean a revision of working hours and the provision of travelling allowances.

3 Surplus labour

A dismissal is due to redundancy if a decline in the volume of trade or work means that an employer requires fewer employees for the existing work, or there is less work for the existing employees; or if the introduction of new business methods or new technology means that fewer employees are required to achieve the same output.

In *Dixon v. Everden*, an employee was informed on her return from holidays that, as the business had operated smoothly with reduced staff, her services were no longer required. It was held that her dismissal was due to redundancy.

In *European Chefs v. Currell*, a pastry cook specialising in making eclairs and meringues was dismissed when his employers decided to discontinue the manufacture of these products and concentrate on the manufacture of continental pastries. He was entitled to a redundancy payment, as the manufacture of these products involved different skills, and his employer's requirements for work of a particular kind had ceased.

In *Haden Ltd v. Cowan*, a divisional contracts surveyor was dismissed by his firm owing to changed economic circumstances. His contract required him to undertake 'any and all duties which reasonably fall within the scope of his capabilities'. It was held that this clause only required him to perform those duties within the scope of his capabilities as a divisional contracts surveyor. As the post had ceased or diminished there was a redundancy situation.

In *Vaux's Brewery v. Ward*, a brewery changed the character of a public house and introduced a discotheque and games room in order to attract a younger clientele. They dismissed a middle-aged barmaid as they wanted a 'bunny-girl' type barmaid as part of the new image. The barmaid was not entitled to a redundancy payment as the nature of the work remained the same.

If an employer seeks to abolish night work in order to concentrate on daytime production, an employee who works night shifts is entitled to a redundancy payment if he refuses the offer of daytime employment. The requirements of the employer for work of a particular kind, i.e. night work, have ceased (*Morrison and Poole v. Ceramic Engineering Ltd*).

An undertaking will often re-organise its working hours in order to achieve maximum efficiency. An employee who does not agree to a variation of his working hours in these circumstances may not be entitled to a redundancy payment. If the exercise is merely a means of discarding surplus labour, there is then an entitlement to a redundancy payment.

In *Johnson v. Nottingham Police Authority*, two clerks were employed to work five days a week from 9.30 to 5.30 p.m. The police authority, seeking to achieve greater efficiency, proposed to introduce six-day working, divided into two shifts of 8 a.m. to 3 p.m., and 1 p.m. to 8 p.m. Both clerks refused to change over to the new system of working and were dismissed. Their dismissal was not due to redundancy as the work remained the same and it was 'the same job done to a different schedule'.

If in the course of a re-organisation an employee is dismissed, the presumption is that the dismissal is not due to redundancy. In *Lesney Products Ltd v. Nolan*, night work at a factory was stopped after a fall in sales. The previous day and evening shift on which overtime was worked was split into two day shifts, on which the equivalent work was done. Employees were offered work on the new day shifts. Those who refused were dismissed and were not entitled to a redundancy payment. The re-organisation of shifts with the loss of overtime did not create a redundancy situation as the employer's requirements remained the same.

If a work force is expanded to meet a scale of production which never materialises as the employer has been over-optimistic in his forecast, this is not a cessation or diminution of work as the work never materialised initially. An employee who is dismissed in these circumstances is not entitled to a redundancy payment (*O'Hare & Rutherford v. Rotaprint Ltd*).

If an employee becomes surplus to requirements in one section of the business and is moved to another section, and in doing so displaces a second employee, that employee will be dismissed for redundancy.

A distinction must be drawn between redundancy and the needs of employees to adapt themselves to new methods and techniques. If an employee fails to adapt, his subsequent dismissal will not be due to redundancy. In *Hindle v. Percival Boats*, the company, who were boat builders, changed from the use of wood to fibreglass in the manufacture of boats. Hindle, a skilled craftsman, was dismissed as 'he was too good and too slow', and therefore unable to adapt to a new technology because of the decline in the use of wood. It was held that the dismissal was not due to redundancy. Similarly in *North Riding Garages v. Butterwick*, a workshop manager failed to adapt to new working methods when new employers took over the business. As there was no change in the nature of the work his subsequent dismissal was not due to redundancy.

Offer of further or alternative employment

An employee will not be entitled to a redundancy payment if he unreasonably refuses an offer by his employer and either: (*a*) the provisions of the renewed contract, or of the new contract as to the capacity and place in which he would be employed, and as to the other terms and conditions of employment would not differ from the corresponding provisions of the previous contract; or (*b*) the terms and conditions differ, but the offer constitutes an offer of suitable employment.

An employee has been held to have had reasonable grounds for refusing an offer of re-engagement when he sold his house (after being given notice), in anticipation of moving to another area.

The alternative employment offered must be suitable. Factors to be considered are the differences as to capacity, terms and conditions of employment, the place of work when compared with the employee's previous employment.

In *Taylor v. Kent CC*, a headmaster was made redundant and was offered a post as a supply teacher. Although there was no reduction in salary, it was held that his refusal was justified in that the consequent loss of status and authority made the offer unsuitable.

In *Ramage v. Harper McKay*, a salesman was offered alternative employment as a warehouse/relief representative. It was held to be unsuitable as it involved not only loss of status, but also loss of bonuses, trade contracts and the use of a car.

In *Standard Telephone Cables v. Yates*, a card wirer for ten years was made redundant and was offered alternative employment as an assembly operator with an associated company taking over the works. It was held to be unsuitable as the work offered was less skilled than her previous work.

If the new employment is at a greater distance than the old from an employee's home, it does not of itself make the new employment unsuitable. Factors which must be considered as a consequence of the additional travelling involved, are the employee's health, age, domestic circumstances, and the time and cost involved in travelling. If the change involves an employee having to move house this might well indicate that the offer is unsuitable.

Employment with an associated employer

If a redundant employee is offered employment with an associated employer then in general the two employers are regarded as the same, and continuity of employment is preserved. If an employee refuses the offer he must, in order to qualify for a redundancy payment, show that the offer was unsuitable. The EPCA provides that 'any two employers are to be treated as associated, if one is a company of which the other (directly or indirectly) has control, or if both are companies of which a third person (directly or indirectly) has control.'

The various area boards of the nationalised industries are not regarded as associated employers, within the meaning given to the phrase by the Act. In *Southern Electricity Board v. Collins*, an employee transferred from the Southern Electricity Board to the Central Electricity Generating Board for six and a half months in 1965. He returned to the SEB until he was made redundant in 1968. It was held that although he had been employed by the SEB since 1951, he was only entitled to three years' redundancy payment as his transfer to the CEGB broke the continuity of employment.

Change of ownership of a business
If there is a change in the ownership of the business, an offer by the new employer to engage the employee on the terms of the old contract or re-engage him under a new contract will be regarded as an offer of renewal. An employee cannot claim a redundancy payment in these circumstances, unless he can show reasonable grounds for refusing the offer.

Where there has been a change of ownership of part of a business, the correct test for redundancy purposes is to determine whether there is a transfer of a going concern, i.e. does it remain the same business in different hands. If there has been a transfer of physical assets, the new owner may use these assets in whatever business he chooses. In *Melon v. Hector Powe Ltd*, the appellants manufactured men's suits. They sold their factory in Scotland to another company which agreed to take over the business and retain most of the employees. It was held that as the purchasing company operated a different business, there was a transfer of certain assets, and the employees were entitled to redundancy payments.

Where a new owner purchases premises and carries on a completely different type of business, or purchases the physical assets of a business, there is no continuity of employment, and employees may claim redundancy payments.

In these circumstances, an employee remining at work, who does not claim a redundancy payment from his former employer, can subsequently only claim a redundancy payment for the time spent with the new employer. In *Woodhouse v. Peter Brotherhood*, a company manufacturing diesel engines sold its factory premises to another company. Some plant and machinery were sold, as the purchasing company manufactured other types of machinery. Employees of the old company who accepted employment with the new company were eventually made redundant by the new company. They were not entitled to count the years spent with the old company in computing their entitlement to a redundancy payment, as there was only a transfer of the physical assets. They would have been eligible for a redundancy payment from their old employers had they applied for payment at the time of the transfer of the assets.

In *Crompton v. Truly Fair Ltd*, a company sold its premises, plant and machinery to another company, and its employees were offered employment in a different capacity, by the new company. As only the physical assets had been transferred, not the business itself, the employees of the old company were entitled to a redundancy payment from the old company, even though they were re-engaged by the new company.

Trial period

An employee, whose contract is renewed on the basis of new terms and conditions is entitled to a trial period of four weeks (or such longer period as may be agreed by the parties for the purpose of retraining the employee), to decide whether the employment is suitable.

The new agreement must be made in writing, before the employee starts work under the renewed or new contract. It must specify the date of the end of the trial period and the terms and conditions of employment which will apply after the end of that period.

During this period both parties are free to terminate the new contract or give notice of termination. In either case the employee will be treated as having been dismissed at the termination of the original contract. However, if the employee, either before or during the trial period, unreasonably terminates the contract, he will not be entitled to a redundancy payment. The burden of proof is on the employer to prove that the employee's conduct was unreasonable in refusing the offer of re-engagement.

An employee is entitled, in certain circumstances, to a common law trial period. This has the effect of prolonging the total trial period to which he or she is entitled.

An employee who is constructively dismissed may be offered new terms by an employer. The employee is entitled to a reasonable period within which to decide whether or not to accept these terms. If he decides not to accept the new contract, he may resign within a reasonable time and claim constructive dismissal. If he accepts the new terms, the statutory trial period will then commence from the time of the acceptance.

In *Air Canada v. Lee*, a switchboard operator agreed to move to her employers' new premises on a trial basis. There was no mobility term in her contract and she gave notice after two months at the new premises. It was held that she had been made redundant, as she had by consent merely postponed the decision as to whether to treat the contract as repudiated. In this case the statutory trial period had never began to run. Her original contract only terminated when she decided, 'before the expiry of the reasonable period of the common law and trial period' that 'she did not wish to continue to be employed'.

In *Turvey v. C. W. Cheney & Sons Ltd,* a polisher was offered work in a different department. The company had no power to insist on the change and indicated that he would take the new work on trial. He decided after more than four weeks that the job was not suitable. It was held that he had been dismissed for redundancy, as he had never in law accepted the new contract, and he had left before the expiry of the reasonable common law trial period.

Dismissal during period of notice

An employee who is dismissed for conduct which justifies summary dismissal (e.g. theft), is not entitled to a redundancy payment. An employee who has been given notice because of redundancy, and who is dismissed for misconduct during that period of notice does not automatically lose his entitlement to a redundancy payment. He may appeal to a tribunal, which has the discretion to award him the full payment, or part of the payment, or no payment as it thinks fit. In *Jarmain v. Pollard*, an employee aged 53 stole scrap from his employers during his period of notice of redundancy and was subsequently convicted of theft. As he had worked for the company for seven years, he was awarded half the redundancy payment he would otherwise have received.

An employee who takes part in a strike during his period of notice, and is dismissed for so doing, is entitled to the payment which would have been due on the expiry of the notice. The employer may request that the employee returns to work after the strike, and remains at work after the date of the expiration of the notice for the number of days which were lost due to the strike. If the employee refuses to do so, and the employer withholds the redundancy payment, the employee may appeal to a tribunal. If the tribunal decides that the employee had reasonable grounds for not complying with the employer's request, it may award the full payment, or part of it, according to the circumstances.

An employee who is on strike and is made redundant is not entitled to a redundancy payment. The EPCA provides that if an employer terminates the contract of employment by reason of the employee's conduct, in circumstances where he is entitled to do so, the employee is not entitled to a redundancy payment.

Departure before notice expires
An employee, given notice terminating his employment, may wish to leave before the notice expires. He may give the employer notice in writing to terminate the contract of employment. If the employer does not object to the employee's premature departure, the employee's entitlement to a redundancy payment is unaffected. If the employer objects, he may serve a written notice on the employee, stating his objection, and requesting the employee to withdraw the notice. The notice must also state that, unless the employee does so, the employer will contest any liability to pay him a redundancy payment. If an employee leaves after such a notice has been served on him, and the employer withholds a redundancy payment, the employee may appeal to a tribunal. The tribunal must examine the case on its merits in order to consider the employee's reason for leaving and the employer's reasons for wanting the employee to stay. It may award the employee the full payment he would have received if notice had been worked, or part of the payment, or no payment.

Lay-off and short-time working

An employer may lay off his employees or put them on short time working if there is insufficient work available for his labour force e.g. a recession or shortage of business. A lay-off occurs where an employee is not entitled to renumeration as the employer does not provide work for him. Short-time working occurs when less than half a week's pay is earned, due to shortage of work.

A lay-off or short-time working may constitute grounds for constructive dismissal unless an employer has reserved the right to do so in the contract of employment. In *Jewell v. Neptune Concrete Ltd*, a labourer who had worked for a company for four years was given his cards by the company, but was told that he was merely laid off. He found other employment, but the first company informed him one month later that his employment was to be resumed. It was held that there had been a dismissal.

An employee, whose employer has retained a contractual right to lay off or put his employees on short time, is nevertheless entitled in certain circumstances to a redundancy payment. He may claim if he has been laid off or put on short time for more than four consecutive weeks, or for at least six weeks in any period of thirteen weeks. The employee must give written notice to the employer, no later than four weeks after the lay off or short time has finished, stating that he intends to claim a redundancy payment.

The employer may agree to the claim, or he may consider that there are reasonable prospects of resuming normal working for at least thirteen weeks, and serve a counter notice to this effect on the employee. If the claim or counter claim is not withdrawn, a tribunal will have to decide whether there were such prospects. An employee is entitled to a redundancy payment if the counter notice is withdrawn by the employer, or the thirteen weeks' employment fails to materialise.

Calculation of redundancy pay

The amount of compensation paid to a redundant employee is calculated on a formula which is based on the employee's age, the amount of his weekly earnings and the length of continuous employment. A similar formula is used to calculate the basic award in a compensation order for unfair dismissal (see page 125).

An employee is entitled to the following amounts for each completed year of employment: one and a half week's pay for each year between the ages of forty-one and sixty-four (men), fifty-nine (women); one week's pay for each year between the ages of twenty-two and forty-one; half a week's pay for each year between the ages of eighteen and twenty-two. Not more than twenty years service may be taken into account and earnings over £145 a week are disregarded in a calculation. The maximum possible payment is therefore $20 \times 1\frac{1}{2} \times £145 = £4350$.

An employee's entitlement is reduced if the redundancy occurs after the sixty-fourth birthday of a male employee or the fifty-ninth birthday of a female employee. The amount is reduced by one-twelfth for each month employed after the age of sixty-four or fifty-nine (as the case may be), e.g. A man earning £100 per week, with thirty years reckonable employment, is made redundant aged sixty-four years, five months. His initial entitlement of £3000 will be reduced by £1250, making his redundancy payment £1750.

The employee's entitlement is computed by reference to a week's pay (see page 70). Most employees have normal working hours and these can be easily ascertained from the written particulars of their terms of employment, together with any relevant working agreement entered into with their employers.

To qualify for a redundancy payment an employee must have the appropriate period of continuous employment (see page 101). Absences due to pregnancy, sickness, holidays, lay offs or short time do not affect continuity as the contract of employment remains in being. Continuity is also maintained in the week(s) when an employee was on strike, or locked out, or on service with the armed forces or employed abroad.

The Redundancy Fund

The Redundancy Fund is financed by an allocation from contributions paid by employers under the Social Security Act. An employer who makes a redundancy payment may claim a rebate from the fund (at present forty-one per cent).

If an employer is insolvent, and therefore unable to make a redundancy payment, the Department of Employment will make a direct payment to an employee. In such a case the Department will seek to recover only the amount of the redundancy payment remaining after the rebate has been allowed.

If an employer refuses, without good reason, to make a redundancy payment, the Department will make a direct payment and will take proceedings to recover the whole sum from the recalcitrant employer.

An employer may claim a rebate if he is liable to make a redundancy payment. If an employer makes a payment in circumstances where he is under no obligation to do so (e.g. because of the employee's conduct; where a claim has been made out of time), he is not entitled to a rebate. If an employer makes a payment in excess of the statutory maximum, he cannot claim a rebate in respect of the excess.

Consultation and the protective award

An employer is required to consult with the appropriate trade union if he proposes to make any of his employees redundant. Notification of his proposals will enable the trade union to examine his plans to see if there is any way of reducing the numbers involved, or mitigating the effects of the redundancies. Consultation is required even where the employees have volunteered for redundancy.

The EPCA sets out minimum periods of consultation, which vary from thirty days for between ten and ninety-nine dismissals, to ninety days for dismissals of a hundred or more employees. The employer must notify the union in writing of the reason for the proposals, the number and descriptions of employees involved, the method of selection, the proposed method of carrying out the redundancies and the dates of dismissal.

If an employer fails, without good reason, to give notice or consult with the appropriate trade union, it may within three months request an industrial tribunal to make a protective award. A protective award requires an employer to pay the employees covered by the award their normal week's pay for a specified period, i.e. the protected period. This period varies from twenty-eight days to ninety days depending on the numbers involved, and will apply to employees whom the employer plans to dismiss, or has already dismissed for redundancy.

An employer who proposes to make redundant more than a hundred employees at one establishment within ninety days, or more than ten employees within thirty days must notify the Secretary of State of his proposals within ninety days, or thirty days respectively. He must also notify the representatives of any trade unions whose members are affected. If he fails to give notice he may be penalised by forfeiting up to $\frac{1}{10}$th of his redundancy rebate or being liable to a fine of up to £400.

10

Discrimination in Employment

There are a number of international conventions which seek to outlaw various discriminatory practices in employment. The International Labour Organisation's Convention (No. 111), which refers to discrimination in Employment and Occupation, requires those ratifying the Convention to take measures against 'any distinction, exclusion or preference made on the basis of race, colour, sex, religion, political opinion, national extraction or social origin, which has the effect of nullifying or impairing equality of opportunity, or treatment in employment or occupation'.

Although the United Kingdom has not ratified Convention No. 111, it has nevertheless ratified the European Social Charter and the European Convention for the Protection of Human Rights and Fundamental Freedom, and in keeping with its obligations, various statutes have been passed which are intended to outlaw discriminatory practices in employment.

Discrimination on the grounds of sex or race

The Sex Discrimination Act 1975 'renders unlawful certain kinds of sex discrimination and discrimination on the grounds of marriage', and establishes a Commission whose function is to work towards the elimination of such discrimination, and to promote 'equality of opportunity between men and women generally'. Although the Act is drafted in terms of unlawful discrimination against women, it is also unlawful to discriminate against men on similar grounds, or against a married person of either sex, solely on the grounds of that person's marital status.

The Race Relations Act 1976 is modelled on the Sex Discrimination Act, and makes 'fresh provision with respect to discrimination on racial grounds, and relations between people of different racial groups'. Discrimination may take three forms: direct discrimination, indirect discrimination, or victimisation.

Direct discrimination
A person discriminates against another if, on the grounds of sex or marital status or race, he treats that person less favourably than he treats or would treat other persons.

In *Skyrail Oceanic Ltd v. Coleman*, the appellant was dismissed by her employers on the day after her marriage to a man who worked in a rival agency. Both employers agreed that there was a risk of disclosure of confidential information, and as the husband was the breadwinner, the wife was dismissed. It was held that the dismissal of a woman based on the assumption that men are most likely to be the main supporters of the family amounts to sex discrimination.

An intention to discriminate must be shown, for if there is some other genuine reason for treating a woman less favourably, this is not discrimination on the grounds of her sex.

Discrimination cannot be justified on the grounds of convenience. In *Hurley v. Mustoe*, a married woman with four young children was refused employment as a waitress. The employer's policy was not to employ persons who had young children, as he had found them unreliable in the past. There was no evidence to suggest that the employer would refuse to employ men with small children, and the employer's policy was therefore held to be discriminatory. Browne-Wilkinson J. stated 'Even if . . . one concedes that some women with small children are less reliable than those without, it does not follow that it is necessary in order to achieve reliability to exclude all women with children'.

In *Horsey v. Dyfed County Council*, a local authority refused secondment to a trainee social worker to attend a course in the London area. Her husband was employed in the London area and the authority was afraid that she would not return to her employment at the end of the course. It was held that the authority had

committed an act of discrimination as it had made a general
assumption about a married woman's behaviour, which could not
be lawfully made.

Evidence of direct racial discrimination is rarely available, and a
tribunal is entitled to draw an inference of discrimination from
indirect evidence.

In *Owen and Briggs v. James*, a coloured girl answered an
advertisement for a typist with a firm of solicitors, but did not obtain
the post. Later she saw a differently worded advertisement and
returned, not realising it was for the same post. She was told not to
come back. The employer made a comment about employing
coloured girls (which was possibly racist) to the successful applicant.
It was held that the solicitors were in breach of the Race Relations
Act.

In *Zarczynska v. Levy*, it was held that a white barmaid who was
dismissed for refusing an order by her employer to apply a colour
bar, could claim that she had been treated less favourably on racial
grounds even though she had not been discriminated against on the
grounds of her race.

Indirect discrimination

This occurs when a requirement or condition is applied to a person
of one sex, or to single persons, or to persons of other racial groups:

1   Which is such that the proportion of the complainant's sex or
    racial group or married persons is considerably smaller than the
    proportion of persons of the other sex, or of another racial group
    or single persons, who can comply with it; and
2   Which cannot be shown to be justifiable irrespective of the sex,
    race or marital status of the person to whom it is applied; and
3   Which is to that person's detriment because he or she cannot
    comply with it.

A complainant must prove the first and second counts, while an
employer must attempt to justify discrimination under the third
count.

There is little authority on what constitutes a requirement or
condition. In *Clarke v. Eley and Eley v. Powell*, it was held that an
agreed redundancy procedure which provided for the dismissal of
part-time employees before full-time employees amounted to a

requirement or condition. This was discriminatory, as the majority of part-time employees were women and a large proportion would be unable to comply with the requirement or condition to work full-time in order to avoid redundancy. The EAT nevertheless stated that the standard of last in first out should be regarded as justifiable, even though its effect is indirectly discriminatory.

In *Steel v. Union of Post Office Workers*, it was conceded that the allocation of postal work by seniority amounted to a 'requirement or condition' (see page 148). In *Price v. Civil Service Commission,* it was alleged that an imposition of an age limit of twenty-eight for a Civil Service post was discriminatory. The applicant was thirty-five, and claimed that women tended to return to work after bearing and rearing children. The words 'can comply with' meant practically possible, not theoretically possible. The case was remitted to an industrial tribunal to determine on statistical evidence whether the proportion of women who could comply was considerably smaller than the proportion of men who could comply, and it was held that the age limit was discriminatory.

In *Hussein v. Saints Complete House Furnishers*, an employer stipulated that he would not interview job applicants who lived in the Liverpool City Centre area, as experience had shown that they attracted their unemployed friends, who stood in front of the shop. He was held to have discriminated indirectly against black and coloured applicants, as fifty per cent of the population of the City Centre area was black or coloured, while outside the area the percentage was two per cent.

An employer who seeks to justify such discrimination must satisfy the burden of proof, i.e. that on the balance of probabilities such discrimination is not merely convenient, but necessary. A tribunal will consider whether the following requirements have been satisfied (Phillips J., in *Steel v. Union of Post Office Workers*):

1 The onus of proof lies on the person asserting the proposition, i.e. the employer;
2 He must satisfy the industrial tribunal that the case is genuine and the requirement or condition is necessary;
3 All the circumstances must be considered, including the discriminatory effect of the requirement or condition if it is permitted to continue;

4   The need for the requirement or condition should be weighed
    against that effect;
5   A requirement or condition considered to be necessary must be
    distinguished from one which is merely convenient. It is relevant
    to consider whether the employer can achieve his object.

Justifiable, when referring to the requirement, means 'reasonably
necessary' or 'right and proper in the circumstances'. In *Ojutiku v.
Manpower Services Commission*, it was held that the Commission's
refusal to sponsor for training persons who lacked managerial
experience was justified by the subsequent inability of those persons
to find jobs, even when trained. The discrimination was therefore
justifiable despite its indirect discriminatory effect on coloured
people.

No award of damages will be made against an employer who fails
to prove that a discriminatory practice was justifiable, if he can show
that the requirement or condition was not applied with the intention
of treating the complainant less favourably.

In *Kingston and Richmond Area Health Authority v. Kaur*, it was
held that it was justifiable for a health authority to require its nurses
to wear a uniform 'without alteration'. A trainee Sikh nurse who
wished to wear trousers under her uniform had therefore not been
discriminated against.

In *Panesar v. Nestlé Company*, it was held that a rule that no
beards were allowed in the chocolate-making part of a factory was
reasonable and that, although the rule was apparently discriminatory as the applicant was a Sikh, it was nevertheless justifiable.

Although the provisions of the Acts are not retrospective, they
will nevertheless apply to acts of a continuing discriminatory nature.
In *Steel v. Union of Post Office Workers*, the Post Office awarded
postal walks according to seniority, which was judged according to
the length of an employee's permanent status. Women had only
been able to attain permanent status since 1975. A walk was given to
a man whose permanent status was longer, but whose total length of
service was shorter than that of the complainant. It was conceded
that the ruling amounted to 'a requirement or condition', and was
discriminatory.

Detriment is defined by its ordinary literal meaning of being
placed at a disadvantage. In *Schmidt v. Austicks Bookshops*, a

company laid down a rule that female employees were not allowed to wear trousers and must wear overalls. A female employee persisted in wearing trousers and was dismissed. She complained that the overall restriction was an unlawful detriment, and that both restrictions were less favourable treatment. It was held that the restriction was not serious enough to be a detriment, and as male employees were not allowed to wear tee shirts, there was no less favourable treatment of female employees.

In *BL Cars v. Brown*, several black employees complained of racial discrimination, as the employers had issued an instruction to the security men at the gates to check the identity of every black employee trying to enter the premises. This followed the arrest of a black employee who had been charged with theft. It was held that the black employees had been unlawfully discriminated against, in that they had been subjected to a detriment.

It is not discrimination on the grounds of sex to dismiss a woman because she is pregnant. As there is no male equivalent of a pregnant woman, it is not possible for a pregnant woman to argue that she is being treated less favourably than a man in her situation (*Turley v. Allders Departmental Stores Ltd*). Her remedy would be to claim for unfair dismissal under Section 60 of the Employment Protection (Consolidation) Act (see page 101).

An employer cannot buy a right to discriminate by paying extra to employees who are the subject of discrimination. In *Ministry of Defence v. Jeremiah*, both male and female examiners were employed at a government ordnance factory. Overtime was voluntary, but any men working overtime had to make colour bursting shells and were paid an extra 4p per hour. This was very dirty work which women were not required to do. It was held that the practice discriminated against the male employees.

Victimisation

It is unlawful to treat a person less favourably than another as that person has brought proceedings, or given evidence, or information, or alleged a contravention of the Sex Discrimination Act, Equal Pay Act or Race Relations Act; or if it is known that a person intends to do any of these things, or it is suspected that she has done, or intends to do any of them. There is no protection if the allegation was false and was not made in good faith.

Discrimination before and during employment

Discrimination before employment

Discrimination *before employment* may occur in any of the following ways:

1 In the arrangements made for the purpose of determining who shall be offered employment; or
2 In the terms on which employment is offered; or
3 By refusing or deliberately omitting to offer employment because of a person's sex or race.

It is lawful for an applicant to be asked questions which might not be asked of a person of the opposite sex, e.g. to ask a married woman if she has plans to start a family.

It is discriminatory if an applicant responds to an advertisement only to be told it is 'man's work' (or woman's work). In *Batisha v. Say and Longleat Enterprises*, a woman applied for the post of cave guide. She was informed that only men would be appointed, but she could attend for the interview if she so wished. The posts had already been filled by local male applicants before she was interviewed. It was held that there had been discrimination, as the posts could have been held by women.

If a woman is not considered for a vacant post because of her sex and the post is not filled, there is nevertheless discrimination (*Roadbury v. Lothian Regional Council*).

In *Grieg v. Community Industry,* two women were employed as a decorating team. When one woman did not turn up for work, the employer refused to allow the other woman to do the work, as there had been problems in the past when there was only one woman in a team. It was held that the employer's motive was irrelevant, as his action was discriminatory.

An employer retains the right to appoint whomsoever he wishes to fill a vacant post. The fact that the appointee is not as well qualified as another applicant is not in itself evidence of discrimination. An employer may therefore use any criteria he so wishes in an appointment, as long as there is no evidence of discrimination on the grounds of sex or race.

Discrimination during employment

Discrimination occurs *during employment* if an employer discriminates, on the grounds of sex or race, against an employee:

1 In affording access to opportunities for promotion, transfer or training or any other benefits, facilities or services or by refusing or deliberately omitting to afford access to them; or
2 In dismissing or subjecting her to any other detriment.

It was held in *Steel v. Union of Post Office Workers* that the Post Office had contravened this provision by refusing to recognise an employee's total length of service as a criterion for promotion and thereby discriminating against women.

In *MacGregor Wallcoverings v. Turton*, the employer's redundancy scheme provided higher rates of pay for employees over the age of sixty. This was held discriminatory, as women employees had to retire at sixty, and were therefore unable to qualify for the higher rates of payment.

Lawful discrimination

Discrimination is permitted under certain circumstances, under the provisions of the Sex Discrimination Act and the Race Relations Act.

1 Discrimination on the grounds of sex

This is permitted in the following circumstances:

(a) Employment for the purposes of a private household;
(b) Employment where the number of employees and those of any associated employer does not exceed five;
(c) Provisions relating to death or retirement;
(d) Where a charitable instrument confers benefit on one sex;
(e) Training for members of one sex by a training body where it appears that at any time, within the twelve months immediately preceding the start of training, there were no persons of that sex holding that post or the numbers are comparatively small;
(f) 'Where being a man is a genuine occupational qualification for the job.' (SDA section 7). This applies in the following circumstances:

     (i)   Which the essential nature of the job calls for a man for reasons of physiology, and for reasons of authenticity in dramatic performances or other entertainments;

    (ii)   When there is a need to preserve decency or privacy, e.g. taking inside leg measurements in a gent's out-fitting department;

   (iii) When the employee is required to live in because of the nature or location of the establishment and there are no separate sleeping or sanitary facilities;

   (iv) Employment in a hospital, prison or other establishment;

    (v)   Employment as a welfare or education counsellor;

   (vi) When there are traditional restrictions on the employment of women, e.g. in mines and quarries;

  (vii) In employment likely to be performed outside the United Kingdom, in a country whose laws or customs preclude a woman from performing those duties;

 (viii) When the job is one of two to be held by a married couple.

(g)   When differentiating between male and female police constables with regard to the requirements for height, uniform, equipment, pensions and the special treatment offered to women in pregnancy and childbirth;

(h)   Provisions relating to the height of prison officers;

(j)   Employment as a minister of religion;

(k)   Employment as a midwife.

In *Timex Corporation v. Hodgson*, an employer selected two male supervisors for redundancy, contrary to company policy of 'last in first out'. A woman supervisor was retained, as she could deal with women's personal problems in addition to her ordinary job. It was held that the employer was not liable, for although there had been discrimination, the sex of the employee was a genuine occupational qualification, as in (f) above.

The SDA provides that nothing in the Act 'shall render unlawful any act done by a person if it was necessary for him to do it in order to comply with a requirement' of earlier legislation, or to safeguard national security. For example, in *Page v. Freight Hire (Tank Haulage) Ltd*, a twenty-three year old woman was employed as an

HGV driver. Her employers refused to allow her to drive loads of a chemical (DMF) which the manufacturers warned was potentially dangerous to women of child-bearing age. It was held that discrimination was lawful, to comply with the Health and Safety at Work Act 1974.

In *Hugh-Jones v. St. John's College, Cambridge*, a woman was barred by college statutes from being appointed a research fellow. As the college statutes had been enacted before 1975, the discrimination was not unlawful.

2 Discrimination on the grounds of race
This is permitted in the following circumstances:

(*a*) Employment for the purposes of a private household;

(*b*) When a charitable instrument confers benefit on one particular racial group;

(*c*) When providing persons of a particular racial group with access to:

  (i) facilities or services to meet their special needs in regard to their education, training or welfare or any ancillary benefits; or

  (ii) facilities and training or encouraging them to take advantage of those opportunities, where during the preceding twelve months there were no persons of that race doing that work or their numbers were comparatively small.

(*d*) When providing persons not ordinarily resident in Great Britain with access to facilities for education or training or ancillary benefits;

(*e*) Where being a member of 'a particular racial group is a genuine occupational qualification for the job'. This applies in the following cases:

 (i) participation in a dramatic performance or other entertainment where authenticity is required;

 (ii) employment as an artist's or photographic model where authenticity is required;

 (iii) employment in a place where food or drink is provided and consumed and a person of that racial group is required for authenticity;

(iv)   provisions of personal welfare services which can be most effectively provided by a person of that racial group.

There is also a provision in the RRA that nothing in the Act will render unlawful any act done by a person if it was necessary to comply with earlier legislation or to safeguard national security.

The Commission for Racial Equality's Code of Practice came into operation on 1 April 1984. The Code gives practical guidance on the provisions of the Race Relations Act, and how to prevent racial discrimination and achieve equality of opportunity.

Advertisements

It is unlawful to publish an advertisement indicating an intention to discriminate. The use of a job description with a sexual or racial connotation, e.g. waiter, salesgirl, postman, stewardess, will be taken as an indication of such an intention, unless the advertisement contains an indication to the contrary.

The publisher of an advertisement which proves to be discriminatory will not be liable to any penalty if he can prove that he relied on a statement that the advertisement was not unlawful and that it was reasonable for him to do so.

It is also unlawful for a person who has authority over another to instruct that person to commit a discriminatory act, or for a person to induce, or attempt to induce a person to commit a discriminatory act. It was held in *Commission for Racial Equality v. Imperial Society of Teachers of Dancing* that a request from the Society to the careers section of Camden School for Girls not to send anyone coloured as a prospective employee was not an attempt to induce and did not therefore contravene the RRA in that respect.

Discrimination by other bodies

Discrimination against contract workers is also unlawful. (A contract worker is an individual who is not employed by the principal, but by another person, who supplies under a contract made with the principal.) The Acts also prevent discrimination by: a partnership of six or more partners; trade unions, employees and workers' organisations; professional and trade associations; qualifying bodies for various trade and professions; vocational training bodies; employment agencies; Manpower Services Commission, and other allied agencies.

Enforcement of legislation

Anti-discrimination legislation may be enforced in two ways:

1 By an individual bringing proceedings before an industrial tribunal;
2 By the Equal Opportunities Commission (EOC) or the Commission for Racial Equality (CRE).

1 Proceedings before a tribunal

An individual must present his complaint within three months of the discriminatory act taking place. An application out of time may be considered if it is just and equitable to do so.

Although the burden of proof rests on the complainant, he is nevertheless given help to obtain information by submitting questions to the respondent on a prescribed form. The respondent is not obliged to reply, but if he fails to do so, or his replies are evasive and equivocal, the tribunal is entitled to infer that he committed an unlawful act.

The EOC and CRE may, at their discretion, give assistance to an individual who is an actual or prospective complainant, if they consider that the case raises a question of principle, or is complex, or it is unreasonable to expect the applicant to deal with the case unaided. The assistance may take the form of advice, procuring or attempting to procure a settlement of the dispute, arranging for legal advice, assistance or legal representation.

A conciliation officer may intervene if requested to do so by both the parties, or if he considers that there is a reasonable prospect of achieving a voluntary settlement of the complaint.

A tribunal may make any of the following orders which it considers just and equitable:

(*a*) An order declaring the right of the parties in relation to the act to which the complaint relates;
(*b*) An award of compensation, subject to a maximum of £7500;
(*c*) A recommendation that the respondent takes, within a

specified period, practicable action to obviate or reduce the adverse effect on the complainant of any act of discrimination to which the complaint relates.

If, without reasonable justification, the respondent fails to comply with a recommendation, a tribunal may increase an order for compensation (up to the maximum amount) or, if no order was made, make such an order.

A person who is dismissed, and who alleges that the dismissal is discriminatory, is more likely to succeed in an action for unfair dismissal. The burden of proof in a case of unfair dismissal rests on the employer and an industrial tribunal may make an order for re-instatement or re-engagement, or may grant compensation if the case is proven (see p.122). A claimant in a discrimination action may be granted damages which may include compensation for injury to feelings. Although a claimant may bring a complaint under both headings, she cannot be awarded double compensation.

2 Proceedings by the appropriate Commission

Each Commission consists of a chairman and up to fourteen members, who are appointed by the Secretary of State on a full-time or part-time basis. The duties of the Commissions are:

(*a*) To work towards the elimination of discrimination;
(*b*) To promote equality of opportunity between men and women and between persons of different racial groups;
(*c*) To review the workings of the Acts, and, if necessary, to draw up and submit proposals for amendment.

The main functions of each Commission are:

(*a*) To conduct formal investigations, and make recommendations in the light of those investigations. A Commission may recommend changes in policy or procedure, or a change in the law.
(*b*) Where an investigation discloses an unlawful practice, a Commission may serve on the party concerned a non-discrimination notice requiring him to cease the practice or otherwise comply with the law. There is a right of appeal within six weeks to an industrial tribunal.
(*c*) If, within five years of the service of a discrimination notice or

a finding of unlawful discrimination by a court or tribunal, it appears to the Commission that unless restrained the respondent is likely to act unlawfully again, it may apply to a County Court for an injunction.

(*d*) To institute proceedings in respect of discriminatory advertisements, instructions to discriminate or pressure to discriminate.

(*e*) To give assistance to individual complainants to prepare their cases.

(*f*) To undertake or assist research and any educational activities.

(*g*) To submit an annual report on its activities.

11

The Settlement of Industrial Disputes

The majority of industrial disputes are settled informally by the parties to the dispute without recourse to any outside agency. Most companies have procedures for dealing with discipline, works practices and redundancies. The EPCA encourages the provision of voluntary procedural agreements in respect of guarantee payments (section 18), unfair dismissal (section 65), and redundancy (section 96).

The *Industrial Relations Code of Practice* gives practical guidance for promoting good industrial relations. It deals with grievance and dispute procedures, and provides that the aim of the procedure should be to settle the grievance fairly and as near as possible to the point of origin. It should be simple and rapid in operation. It divides disputes into two kinds:

1   Disputes of *right*, which relate to the application or interpretation of existing agreements or contracts of employment;
2   Disputes of *interest*, which relate to claims by employees or proposals by management about terms and conditions of employment.

The Code recommends that the procedure for settling collective disputes should: be in writing; state the level at which a dispute should be raised; lay down time limits for each stage of the procedure; and preclude all forms of industrial action until all stages of the procedure have been concluded and a failure to agree has been formally recorded.

The procedure should also follow three stages:

1 Employee representatives should raise the disputed issue with the management at the level directly concerned.
2 If settlement is not achieved, it should be referred to a higher level within the establishment.
3 If still unresolved it should be referred to further agreed stages e.g. a higher level within the undertaking, or an industry wide procedure.

The Code also refers to arbitration and independent conciliation as a means of settling all types of disputes. It specifically mentions arbitration by The Industrial Arbitration Board or other independent arbitrators as particularly suitable for settling disputes of right, and its wider use for that purpose is desirable. When used, the parties should undertake to be bound by such awards.

ACAS has also issued a Code dealing with Disciplinary Practice and Procedures in Employment. This gives detailed and practical guidance on how to draw up disciplinary rules and procedures, and how to operate them.

Various machinery has been set up by statute to resolve industrial disputes. An individual in dispute with his employer may apply for relief to an industrial tribunal and on appeal to the Employment Appeal Tribunal. Other bodies such as ACAS fulfill a variety of roles in the field of industrial relations, while the Central Arbitration Committee acts as a permanent arbitration body.

Industrial tribunals

Industrial tribunals were first established under the Industrial Training Act 1964. Since that time, their jurisdiction has steadily increased and they now have very wide jurisdiction under various employment statutes. The Donovan Commission described the function of tribunals as providing employers and employees with an easily accessible, speedy, informal and inexpensive procedure for the settlement of their disputes.

Jurisdiction
Industrial tribunals now have jurisdiction in these cases: imposition of industrial training levy (Industrial Training Act 1982); disputes over dock work (Docks and Harbour Act 1966); effect of equality

clause (Equal Pay Act 1970); appeals against notices of health and safety inspectorate (Health and Safety at Work Act 1974); discrimination on grounds of sex or marital status (Sex Discrimination Act 1975); racial discrimination (Race Relations Act 1976); Employment Protection (Consolidation) Act 1978; exclusion or expulsion from trade union (Employment Act 1980); and other Acts under which compensation may be awarded for loss of office.

The Employment Protection (Consolidation) Act 1978, as befits its title, deals with the various rights of parties to a contract of employment. It also provides that disputes relating to the following may be referred to an industrial tribunal: guarantee payments; maternity pay; time off – for trade union duties, for public duties, for looking for work or for making arrangements for further training; unfair dismissal; written statements of reasons for dismissal; provision of written particulars of employment, and itemised pay statements; redundancy payments and rebates.

Tribunals have also been given jurisdiction under this Act over claims for damages for breach of contract of employment, i.e. wrongful dismissal, but as yet no order has been made to bring this provision into operation.

Administration
Separate Central Offices of Industrial Tribunals have been established in London, Glasgow and Belfast for England and Wales, Scotland and Northern Ireland respectively, dealing with the appointment of personnel and the processing of applications. The principal administrative officer for each Central Office is known as the Secretary of Tribunals.

Regional Offices have been established at sixteen centres throughout England and Wales. Each has an Assistant Secretary who deals with the administration of applications, after their initial registration at the Central Office. Industrial tribunals sit at numerous centres within each region, and an average of sixty tribunals sit in England and Wales on each working day.

Composition
Each tribunal consists of a Chairman (a barrister or solicitor of at least seven years standing) and two lay members. Each has an equal voice in the decision reached by the tribunal. A Clerk is also

attached to each tribunal, who advises and assists the parties and the tribunal, before and during the hearing.

Procedure

Proceedings are commenced by the applicant submitting an originating application, in writing, to the Secretary of Tribunals. This sets out the applicant's name and address, the respondent's name and address and the grounds on which relief is sought. It is unnecessary to state what relief is sought, as this allows the tribunal discretion as to what relief (if any) to grant the applicant.

The Secretary of Tribunals enters details of the application in the register and sends a copy of the application to the respondent, together with details of how the respondent may enter an appearance and contest the applicant's claim. If the respondent intends to enter an appearance, he must inform the Secretary within fourteen days of receiving his copy of the originating application, of his intention to do so and on what grounds. A copy of this must be sent to the applicant.

Either party (or the tribunal) may require further particulars of any ground relied on together with any relevant facts, and may require the attendance of any person (including a party to the proceedings) as a witness. Discovery of documents may be granted and an order may be made for the production of any relevant documents.

A tribunal may, on the application of either party, (or of its own accord) convene a pre-hearing assessment. If at this stage it considers that the originating application is unlikely to succeed, or that a particular contention made by one of the parties is without merit, it may advise the party concerned that to proceed with the application or to reassert the contention would lead to an order for costs.

Each party must be given at least fourteen days notice of the hearing, which takes place in public, unless the tribunal considers that a private hearing is appropriate in the circumstances.

A private hearing is only considered appropriate in cases where disclosure would involve matters of national security; contravene any enactment; expose a confidential relationship; or cause substantial injury to an undertaking other than in respect of collective bargaining.

The tribunal may conduct a hearing in such a manner as it

considers most appropriate to the just handling of the proceedings, and to the clarification of the issues before it. A tribunal's proceedings are fairly informal and it is not bound by the strict legal rules relating to the admissability of evidence.

At the hearing, a party and any person entitled to appear may appear in person and has the right to be represented by Counsel, or by a solicitor, or by a trade union or employers' association representative, or by any other person whom he desires to represent him. A party to the proceedings may give evidence, question witnesses and address the tribunal. A witness may be required to give evidence on oath or affirmation. If a party fails to appear, or is not represented at the hearing, the tribunal may, if that party is an applicant, dismiss or dispose of the application in the absence of that party or may adjourn the hearing to a later date.

The tribunal's decision is recorded in a document, which is then sent to the Secretary of Tribunals. He enters the decision in the Register and sends a copy of the entry to each party. In the majority of cases the tribunal gives its decision, and the reasons for arriving at that decision, at the end of the hearing. If it is not possible to give a decision immediately, the tribunal will reserve its decision, and the parties will be notified at a later date.

A tribunal may in limited circumstances review its decision. It may do so if:

1 The decision was wrongly made as a result of an error on the part of the tribunal staff;
2 A party did not receive notice of the proceedings;
3 The decision was made in the absence of a party or a person entitled to be heard;
4 New evidence has become available since the making of the decision;
5 The interests of justice require such a review.

Award of costs

An award will not normally be made in respect of any costs or expenses incurred by either party, but if the tribunal considers that a party has acted vexatiously, frivolously or unreasonably in bringing or conducting proceedings, then it may make an award of costs. It may make an order for that party to pay the whole or part of the other party's costs, or it may order that party to pay to the Secretary of the State part or the whole of any sum paid as allowances to the other party. It may also award costs where a hearing has been postponed or adjourned on the application of one of the parties. Costs will be awarded against an employer:

1 Where a postponement or adjournment has been caused by the employer; or
2 Where an applicant has expressed a wish to be reinstated or re-engaged, and this has been communicated to the employer at least seven days before the hearing; or
3 Where the proceedings have arisen out of the employer's failure to allow an employee to return to work after an absence due to pregnancy or confinement.

Conciliation

The Secretary must, in all cases where an enactment provides for conciliation, inform the parties that the services of a conciliation officer are available to them. A copy of a complaint presented to an industrial tribunal must also be sent to the conciliation officer.

A conciliation officer may offer his services to a party to a dispute before a complaint is lodged. As his aim is to promote a settlement, he may where appropriate encourage the parties to use any other procedures which are available for the settlement of grievances.

Conciliation officers are given specific functions when a complaint of unfair dismissal is presented to an industrial tribunal. A copy of the complaint is sent to a conciliation officer, who must endeavour to promote a settlement without recourse to an industrial tribunal, if requested to do so by either party, or if he considers that he has a reasonable prospect of success. If the employee is no longer employed by the employer, the conciliation officer must seek to promote the employee's reinstatement or re-engagement on terms which appear to the conciliation officer to be equitable. Where the employee does not wish to be reinstated or re-engaged, or where those remedies are not practical, and both parties wish him to act, the conciliation officer may seek to promote agreement as to the amount of compensation to be paid by the employer. The parties may also promote a settlement in that they may agree, in writing, upon the terms of a decision to be made by the tribunal.

In 1983, 35 890 applications were registered in England and Wales. Of these, 72.9% were on the grounds of unfair dismissal, 9.3% on redundancy payments, 5.5% on unfair dismissal payments, 3.5% on equal pay, 4.8% on employment protection, 0.9% on sex discrimination, 1.5% on race relations, while the remainder dealt with contracts of employment, health and safety, industrial training levy and compensation for loss of office.

Of the unfair dismissal applications dealt with in the UK in 1983, 65.2% were settled by agreement between the parties, or withdrawn. The remaining 34.8% were heard by a tribunal, and the applicant was successful in 30% of these cases. The applicant was re-instated or re-engaged in 1.1% of cases, and in most other successful cases compensation was awarded.

Employment Appeal Tribunal

The Employment Appeal Tribunal was established under the Employment Act 1975, and is a superior court of record. It consists of High Court Judges and lay members who are required to have special knowledge or experience of industrial relations, either as employer's or employees' representatives. One of the judges is nominated as the President of the Appeal Tribunal.

The tribunal may sit at any time and in any place in Great Britain, either as a single tribunal or in two or more divisions concurrently. When sitting as a single tribunal, it consists of a judge and either two or four appointed members, equally representative of employers and employees.

Jurisdiction

It considers appeals on questions of law from the findings of industrial tribunals under the Equal Pay Act 1970, the Sex Discrimination Act 1975, the Employment Protection Act 1975, the Race Relations Act 1976, the Employment Protection (Consolidation) Act 1978 and the Employment Act 1980. An appeal may be made on one of the following grounds:

1   The tribunal misdirected itself in law, or misunderstood or misapplied the law.
2   The tribunal's findings are in conflict with the evidence.
3   The decision was such that no reasonable tribunal could have reached it.

An appeal can also be based on a question of fact or law from a decision of a tribunal relating to unreasonable exclusion or expulsion from a trade union. The tribunal also hears appeals, on questions of law, from the decisions of the Certification Officer in respect of objections by trade union members to contributing to the union's political funds; the application of trade union funds for political purposes; the provision of ballots to approve union rules; complaints in respect of resolutions passed in cases involving the amalgamation of trade unions or transfer of engagements from one trade union to another.

An appeal also lies to the Appeal Tribunal from a Certification Officer's ruling that a trade union is not independent, and his refusal to enter a trade union or an employer's association, in the lists of trade unions and employer's associations. An appeal on those grounds may be made on questions of fact or law.

Procedure

The appeal must be lodged within forty-two days of the date on which the decision or order appealed against was sent to the appellant. The notice of appeal must give particulars of the decision appealed against, the questions of law involved, and the grounds of appeal. If it appears to the Registrar of the Appeal Tribunal that the grounds of appeal are not within the Appeal Tribunal's jurisdiction, he must notify the appellant of this fact, and no further action may be taken on the appeal. The appellant may in these circumstances serve a fresh notice of appeal within twenty-eight days of the Registrar's notification, or before the expiration of the forty-two days. He may also express his dissatisfaction, in writing, with the Registrar's decision and the Registrar must then place the papers before a judge or the President for his direction.

On receiving notice of appeal, the Registrar seals the notice with the Appeal Tribunal's seal. He then serves a sealed copy on the appellant and the respondent, and the Secretary of Industrial

Tribunals in the case of an appeal from an industrial tribunal. A notice is served on the Certification Officer in a case involving an appeal from any of his decisions.

If the respondent wishes to contest the appeal, or cross-appeal, he may do so by delivering his answer, or his cross-appeal, in writing, to the Appeal Tribunal. The appellant may, in reply to a cross-appeal, set out the grounds on which he relies. The Registrar will provide copies of the answers and replies to a cross-appeal to the other parties.

If the respondent does not wish to contest an appeal, the parties may deliver to the Appeal Tribunal an agreed draft of an order allowing the appeal. The Tribunal may, if it approves, make an order allowing the appeal on the agreed terms.

The Registrar informs the parties of the arrangements for the hearing. Provision is made for holding a meeting for directions, prior to the hearing, if it appears that this would facilitate the future conduct of the proceedings.

If, at any stage of the proceedings, it appears to the Appeal Tribunal that there is a reasonable prospect of an agreement being reached between the parties, it may take such steps as it thinks fit to enable the parties to avail themselves of any opportunities for conciliation.

The hearings are in public, but the Appeal Tribunal may sit in private, in similar circumstances to those in which an industrial tribunal may conduct its proceedings in private (see page 161). It may order the attendance of witnesses and compel the production of documents. Costs may only be awarded if it appears that the proceedings were unnecessary, improper, vexatious, or there has been unreasonable delay or unreasonable conduct in bringing or conducting the proceedings.

The Appeal Tribunal may, either of its own accord or on the application of a party, review any order made by it. It may, after review, revoke or vary that order on the grounds that:

1   The order was wrongly made as the result of an error on the part of the Tribunal or its staff; or
2   A party did not receive a proper notice of the proceedings leading to the order; or
3   The interests of justice require such review.

A clerical mistake in any order, due to an accidental slip or omission may at any time be corrected by, or on the authority of, a judge or member.

Advisory, Conciliation and Arbitration Service (ACAS)

ACAS was established in 1974, and is charged with the general duty of promoting the improvement of industrial relations. In particular, it is intended to encourage the extension of collective bargaining, and the development and reform of collective bargaining machinery.

Composition

Its work is directed by a Council, which consists of a full-time Chairman and nine other members. Three of the members represent employers' organisations, three are representatives of workers' organisations, whilst the remainder are independent members. All appointments are made by the Secretary of State, who may appoint a further two members, and up to three full-time or part-time deputy chairmen. The appointments will be for an initial term of five years, and may be renewed for a further term.

The Council may, with the approval of the Secretary of State, appoint a Secretary and such other officers and servants as may be necessary for its work. It may maintain such offices in those major centres of employment in Great Britain as it thinks fit for the purpose of discharging its functions. Although its functions are performed on behalf of the Crown, it is not subject to directions of any kind from any Minister of the Crown as to the manner in which it exercises any of its functions. These functions are: collective conciliation, arbitration, mediation, advice, industrial conciliation, and inquiry.

Collective conciliation

ACAS may offer its assistance to the parties when a trade dispute exists, or is apprehended, in order to bring about a settlement. This may be at the request of the employer and/or the trade union concerned, or the approach may be made on the initiative of ACAS.

The essential characteristic of conciliation is its voluntary nature. As the settlement of dispute is a matter for the parties themselves to resolve, the involvement of ACAS is only requested when the parties have exhausted their own procedures for the settlement of disputes without resolving the dispute; or when the parties agree that overriding considerations require the services of a conciliator. All agreements subsequently reached in conciliation are the responsibility of the parties in dispute.

During 1982, ACAS received more than 1800 requests for collective conciliation. More than 60% related to pay and the terms and conditions of employment, while the remainder dealt with dismissal, discipline and redundancy.

Arbitration

Three conditions must be fulfilled before ACAS may refer a dispute to arbitration. The consent of each of the parties must be obtained; the agreed procedures for settling disputes must have been used and have failed to produce a settlement; and the likelihood of an agreement being reached by conciliation must have been considered and rejected.

There are three modes of arbitration, namely the use of a single arbitrator, the appointment of a special board of arbitration and reference to the Central Arbitration Committee.

A single arbitrator is appointed by ACAS from a panel of experienced arbitrators. This method is speedy and confidential and is especially suitable for the settlement of local disputes.

Boards of arbitration are usually set up for the larger or more significant disputes. The board consists of an independent chairman, appointed by ACAS and an equal number of members, representing employer and trade union interests in the dispute. The parties to the dispute are asked to agree that, if the members of the board fail to reach unanimous agreement on their award, the Chairman will have the full powers of an umpire to decide the matter. Both a single arbitrator and a board may call upon the services of assessors to provide professional or expert knowledge where technical or complex matters are in issue. Assessors take no part in the award-making process.

Central Arbitration Committee   ACAS may refer a dispute to the

Central Arbitration Committee (CAC) at the request of the parties to the dispute (see page 171). The CAC is a permanent arbitration tribunal and consists of a Chairman and members representative of employees' and employers' interests. The Chairman has the powers of an umpire where the Committee fails to reach a unanimous decision.

Mediation

Mediation is another method of helping to resolve disputes. It is mid-way between conciliation and arbitration, in that the mediator commences by way of conciliation, but nevertheless formulates proposals or recommendations, which the parties may accept, or use as a basis for negotiations which will lead to a settlement.

As the parties are not bound to accept the mediator's proposals or recommendations, it is an acceptable format where the parties are unwilling to commit themselves to arbitration and a binding award. A single mediator or a board of mediation may be appointed, and all such appointments are from outside ACAS.

Advice

ACAS also provides free advice to employers, employers' associations, employees and trade unions on various aspects of industrial relations and employment policies. It offers a wide range of services including advisory visits to firms, conducting diagnostic and other surveys, instituting projects, organising seminars and conferences, and setting up working parties to examine deep seated industrial relations problems.

Industrial conciliation

ACAS conciliation officers are under a statutory obligation to endeavour to settle complaints made by individuals alleging infringement of certain employment rights. A copy of a complaint presented to an industrial tribunal must also be sent to a conciliation officer who must seek to resolve the complaint without recourse to a tribunal hearing. Some 38% of the individual conciliation cases received by ACAS in 1982 were settled by conciliation, 3% were settled privately, 22% were withdrawn, while 32% were heard by a tribunal.

Inquiry

ACAS may inquire into any question relating to industrial relations generally, or in a particular industry, undertaking or part of an undertaking. The results of the inquiry may be published, if considered desirable, after sending a draft of the findings to the parties and taking account of their views.

The Service also has an important function in relation to wages councils. At the request of the Secretary of State, it examines questions relating to the abolition or variation of scope of an existing wages council or the establishment of a new wages council. It also examines the development of joint machinery in wages councils, the general operation of wages council legislation, as well as the evolution of wages councils into statutory joint industrial councils.

Codes of practice

ACAS may issue Codes of Practice containing practical guidance for employers and trade unions, with the object of promoting the improvement of industrial relations. Every code must be published initially in a draft form, and any representations as to its content must be considered before its eventual publication. It must also be approved by both Houses of Parliament.

Three Codes of Practice have been issued dealing with: disciplinary practice and procedures in employment, disclosure of information to trade unions for the purposes of collective bargaining, and time off for trade union duties and activities.

Central Arbitration Committee (CAC)

The Committee is a permanent, independent arbitration body maintained at the Crown's expense, but not subject to any directions from any Minister of the Crown as to the way in which it exercises any of its functions.

Composition

It consists of a Chairman, a Deputy Chairman and two panels consisting of members with experience as employers' or employees' representatives. Each member has experience of industrial relations and arbitration and is appointed for an initial term of five years.

Cases are usually heard by a committee of three, consisting of a Chairman and two members, drawn from each panel. The Committee may however sit in two or more divisions with such membership as the Chairman directs, and may be advised by assessors.

Jurisdiction
The Committee fulfills a traditional role as an arbitration body, with its origins in the Industrial Court, set up in 1919. It may arbitrate in any matter relating to a trade dispute, if one party so requests and the other party (or parties) agree. The dispute must have been initially referred to ACAS, who must have concluded that conciliation or the existing dispute procedures could not produce a satisfactory agreement.

The Committee may arbitrate, at the request of one party, in three situations:

1   The Secretary of State may request the Committee to determine whether an employer in receipt of government contracts is observing the Fair Wages Resolution. The concept of fair wages, with powers of referral to the Committee is now contained in a number of statutes, e.g. The Public Passenger Vehicle Act 1981, The Broadcasting Act 1981.

2   An independent recognised trade union may present a complaint that an employer has failed to disclose certain information necessary for collective bargaining. If the Committee finds the complaint justified, it makes a declaration as to what information is to be disclosed. If the employer refuses to comply, a claim may then be made to the Committee for improved terms and conditions for those employees.

3   The Committee may amend any collective agreement, employee pay structure or wage regulation order which contains a provision applying to men or women only. In such a case, reference may be made to the Committee by any party to a collective agreement, by the employer concerned in the pay structure, or in all cases by the Secretary of State.

Procedure
The Committee is not bound by precedent, but nevertheless seeks to achieve consistency in its decisions. The parties are invited to

submit and exchange evidence before the hearing. The procedure at the hearing seeks to avoid the formality of a court of law, by amplification of the written evidence, by explanation, question and discussion, rather than by examination and cross-examination of witnesses. A hearing may be adjourned if it appears that the parties may be able to reach an agreement on their own, or with the aid of conciliation, and they are prepared to try to do so. Costs are not awarded.

Although the parties usually agree on the terms of reference and undertake to honour any award made, an award does not bind the parties in law.

The Committee does not usually inform the parties at the hearing of its decision. They are notified in writing of the decision in a report which also contains an indication of the considerations which have led to the decision. The report may also contain advice or comments which may be of assistance to the parties. Voluntary arbitration cases are held in private and the awards will not be published, unless the parties wish otherwise.

12

Trade Unions

Definition

A trade union is defined in section 28.1 of TULRA as an organisation (whether permanent or temporary) which either:

(a) Consists wholly or mainly of workers of one or more descriptions, and is an organisation whose principal purposes include the regulation of relations between workers of that description or those descriptions and employers' associations; or

(b) consists wholly or mainly of:
  (i)   constituent or affiliated organisations which fulfil the conditions specified in paragraph (a) above (or themselves consist wholly or mainly of constituent or affiliated organisations which fulfil those conditions); or
  (ii) representatives of such constituent or affiliated organisations;

and in either case is an organisation whose principal purposes include the regulation of relations between workers and employers, or between workers and employers' associations, or include the regulation of relations between its constituent or affiliated organisations.

An employer's association is defined in similar terms in section 28.2 of TULRA.

Status

Section 2 of TULRA defines the status of a trade union in the following terms:

1   It is capable of making contracts.
2   All trade union property must be vested in trustees in trust for the union.
3   It is capable of suing and being sued in its own name.
4   Criminal proceedings may be brought against it in its own name.
5   Any judgment, order or award made in proceedings against a trade union in enforceable against its trust property.

A rule or purpose of a trade union is not unlawful or unenforceable by reason only that such a rule or purpose is in restraint of trade. The status of an employers' association is similarly defined in Section 3 of TULRA.

Classification

1   Listed trade union

An organisation of workers which satisfies the statutory definition of a trade union has the legal status of a trade union. It is therefore entitled to have its name entered on the list of trade unions. The list is kept by the Certification Officer and is available for public inspection, free of charge, at all reasonable hours. It also includes the names of organisations registered as trade unions under earlier legislation, organisations affiliated to the TUC, and organisations formed by amalgamations of organisations previously registered as trade unions. The fact that an organisation is included in this list is evidence that it is a trade union and that it is entitled to a certificate stating that it is listed.

One advantage of obtaining this certificate is that the trade union is entitled to certain tax exemptions on its provident fund income. The issue of a certificate is the first step in obtaining a certificate of independence.

The Certification Officer may remove a trade union from the list if requested to so by the organisation. He may also remove an organisation from the list if it appears to him that it is not a trade union, or if he is satisfied that the organisation has ceased to exist.

There is a right of appeal to the Employment Appeal Tribunal against a decision of the Certification Officer.

2 Independent trade unions

A listed trade union may apply to the Certification Officer for a certificate that it is independent. It must show (*a*) that it is not under the domination or control of an employer or a group of employers or of one or more employers' associations, and (*b*) that it is not liable to interference by an employer or any such group or association (arising out of the provision of financial or material support or by any other means whatsoever) tending towards such control.

The larger unions have little difficulty in satisfying these criteria. The smaller unions, especially staff associations, must be looked at very closely to see whether that degree of independence exists.

The decision as to whether a trade union is independent is taken by the Certification Officer after consultation with other interested parties, e.g. other trade unions. The decision is subject to a right of appeal, on a question of law or fact, to the Employment Appeal Tribunal.

Factors to be taken into consideration by the Certification Officer in deciding whether a union is independent include:

1 The degree of participation (if any) of the company's senior management in the union's affairs, and the restrictions (if any) placed on that participation;
2 The financial independence of the union, i.e. its non-dependence on the employer;
3 The facilities provided by the employer, and the effect on the union of a withdrawal of those facilities;
4 Its record of collective bargaining with the employer and its status in disputes procedures;
5 Its membership base, e.g. a union composed entirely of employees of a single company is more likely to be influenced or dominated by that employer.

An independent trade union has certain advantages:

(*a*) Its representatives are entitled to receive information for bargaining purposes and to be informed and consulted in cases of redundancy and under the Transfer of Undertakings (Protection of Employment) Regulations 1981.

(b)   Employees who are members of independent trade unions, are entitled to time off for trade union activities. Employees who are officials of such unions are entitled to time off work (with pay) in order to undertake industrial relations training.

(c)   Employees have a right to join an independent trade union and take part in its activities. A union member who claims that he was dismissed for trade union membership may apply for interim relief.

(d)   The union may enter into a union membership agreement.

(e)   It may obtain payments from the Certification Officer in order to hold secret ballots. It may also use an employer's premises to hold a ballot.

(f)   It may appoint safety representatives from amongst the employees.

(g)   It is entitled to be consulted about contracting out of occupational pension schemes.

3   Recognised trade union

An independent trade union must be recognised by the employer for the purposes of collective bargaining in order to enjoy certain rights conferred by statute. A recognised trade union is entitled to: receive bargaining information; be consulted on impending redundancies; appoint safety representatives; and be notified and consulted with regard to company pension schemes. Its members are also entitled to time off work for union duties and activities.

4   Special register bodies

These are organisations whose names were entered on the special register maintained under the Industrial Relations Act 1971. They consist of companies registered under the Companies Act 1948 or incorporated by charter or letters patent, e.g. British Medical Association, Royal College of Nursing.

Although these organisations are principally concerned with the maintenance and advancement of professional standards and training, they nevertheless take an active interest in the regulation of industrial relations.

The main difference between these bodies and other trade unions is that a special register body is a corporate body, while a trade union may not register under the Companies Acts. Special register bodies enjoy certain immunities granted to other trade unions in respect of tort, actions in tort and the doctrine of restraint of trade. Unlike other trade unions, they are not obliged to keep accounting records, to audit their accounts, or to submit annual returns.

Union rules

The rules of a trade union are set out in its rule book and constitute a binding contract between the union and its members. A member is therefore entitled to enforce a union's rules, and to sue the union's officials if they are in breach of the rules.

The courts have recognised the fact that the rules are not the only source of the agreement between the union and its members. It was stated in *Heaton's Transport v. TGWU* that 'it is not to be assumed that all the terms of the agreement are to be found in the rule book alone; particularly as respects the discretion conferred by the members upon committees or officials of the union as to the way in which, they may act on the union's behalf' (per Lord Wilberforce).

In drafting its rules, a union is free to decide whom it will admit to membership, subject to certain limited exceptions. It may also impose any qualification it deems necessary for membership.

In *Boulting v. ACTAT*, a trade union sought to recover arrears of subscriptions from the plaintiffs, who had been members of the union, but had ceased to pay their subscriptions. The plaintiffs, who were managing directors of a film company, sought an injunction against the union as they contended that they were ineligible for membership in that they were directors and producers. It was held that they were eligible for membership as they exercised the functions of employees on the production floor.

Although the courts strictly interpret the rules relating to the procedural and substantive requirements for membership, a rule will not be regarded as invalid solely on the basis of its arbitrary character. In *Faramus v. Film Artistes' Association*, a union rule provided that a person with a criminal record was ineligible for membership. The plaintiff at the age of seventeen had been convicted of a criminal offence during the German occupation of the

Channel Islands, but had not disclosed this fact. It was held that he was not a member of the union as he had never been eligible for membership. As more than four times as many people sought employment as film extras as there were jobs 'the rules as to admission of membership must inevitably be in some degree arbitrary'.

A trade union is subject to the following Statutory limitations:

1   The rules must contain a term giving a member the right to terminate his membership on giving reasonable notice and complying with any reasonable conditions.
2   The rules must not discriminate against a person on the grounds of sex or race with regard to the terms on which a trade union is prepared to admit that person to membership, or by refusing or deliberately omitting to accept that person's application for membership.
3   The rules must not discriminate against a person on the grounds of being an EEC national.
4   Where an employer operates a union membership agreement, (a 'closed shop'), a person who is employed by that employer or who seeks such employment has the right 'not to have an application for membership of a specified trade union unreasonably refused' and 'not to be unreasonably expelled from a specified trade union'.

The question of reasonableness must be determined in accordance with equity and the substantial merits of the case. A union will not be regarded as having acted reasonably only if it has acted in accordance with its rules or unreasonably if it acted in contravention of its rules.

At common law, the courts have adopted a broad approach to the construction of a union's rules, looking to the intent and purpose of the rule, rather than seeking legal precision and clarity.

'Trade union rule books are not drafted by parliamentary draftsmen. Courts of law must resist the temptation to construe them as if they were; for that is not how they would be understood by the members who are the parties to the agreement of which the terms, or some of them, are set out in the rule book or how they would be and in fact were understood by the experienced members of the Court.' (Lord Wilberforce in *Heaton's Transport v. TGWU*.)

The courts may therefore take into account the customs and practices of a union, as long as they do not conflict with a union rule. In the case of such a conflict, the rule will prevail. In *Heaton's Transport v. TGWU*, the court considered the scope and authority of a shop steward in the light of customary practice, as the union's rules were unclear on this matter.

The courts have always strictly scrutinised those rules which affect a member's livelihood, in particular those concerned with discipline and expulsion.

A trade union cannot exclude the courts as final arbitrators in questions of law. Although a union rule may provide that the internal remedies in the rules must be exhausted before a member can apply to the courts, the courts are not bound by such a provision. In this situation the member must show a reason why he should not initially exhaust the domestic remedies. If there is no such express requirement, the courts will more readily intervene before the internal remedies have been exhausted. In general, the courts will leave matters of fact and discretion initially to the union's appeals procedure, but if a question of law is involved, the courts may intervene at any stage of the proceedings.

The courts may intervene before the commencement of disciplinary proceedings, if it can be shown that no reasonable tribunal, acting in good faith, could uphold the complaint. In *Esterman v. NALGO*, a member disobeyed a union order not to volunteer to assist in certain local government elections. She obtained an injunction to prevent her branch committee from considering whether her conduct was such as to render (her) unfit for membership, as the court considered that on the facts of the case it would be impossible to convict a member of such a charge.

Discipline

A trade union in exercising a disciplinary function is acting in a quasi-judicial capacity. It must therefore abide by the rules of *natural justice* and a failure to observe these rules will render any disciplinary actions void.

1 A member must be given *notice of the charges* levelled against him, of the rule which it is alleged that he has broken, and of the

penalties which could be applied if the charge is proven. He must also be allowed sufficient time to prepare a defence.

In *Lawlor v. Union of Post Office Workers*, the plaintiff and other members of a district council of the union refused to give an assurance to the general secretary of the union that they would discontinue advocating a policy which was in contradiction of official union policy. The executive council of the union followed the general secretary's recommendation and expelled Lawlor and his colleagues from the union. The expulsion was set aside, for although the executive council were given a power of expulsion, Lawlor and his colleagues had not been informed in advance that disciplinary action against them was pending and so had not been given an opportunity to present their case to the executive council.

If during the proceedings the union wish to vary the charges or bring fresh charges against a member, the process must re-commence. In *Annamunthodo v. Oilfield Workers Union*, the appellant was charged with four offences in breach of the union rules. None of the rules gave power to expel the appellant. He attended the initial hearing of the union's General Council and denied the charges. The hearing was adjourned, but he did not attend the adjourned hearing. He was later notified that he had been convicted of all charges and had been expelled under another rule to which no reference had been made in the original charges. It was held that to proceed under an additional rule at the adjourned hearing, without adjourning to give the appellant notice, was contrary to natural justice and the expulsion was invalid.

2 A member must be given the opportunity to be heard by the committee making the decision and must be given a reasonable opportunity of answering the charges (*Annamunthodo v. Oilfield Workers' Union*). The hearing must be fairly conducted, and the union officials must act in good faith and must not pre-judge the issues before the hearing.

In *Roebuck v. National Union of Mine Workers*, the plaintiff was disciplined by the union for allegedly misleading the union's solicitors in a case involving the Yorkshire area president. The disciplinary proceedings were chaired by the area president, who had initiated the proceedings and had earlier expressed a view concerning the member's guilt. It was held that the disciplinary proceedings were void.

In *Taylor v. National Union of Seamen*, the plaintiff was dismissed by the union's general secretary for insubordination. He appealed against the dismissal to the executive council. The general secretary chaired the meeting, and after the plaintiff had withdrawn, the meeting was treated to various statements which were not the subject of the charge, but were prejudicial to the plaintiff. It was held that as the plaintiff had no opportunity of rebutting these statements, the hearing was in breach of the rules of natural justice.

Expulsion

The power to expel a member must be expressly reserved in a union rule book, as such a right cannot be implied in the rules.

In *Spring v. National Amalgamated Stevedores & Dockers Society*, a union had admitted to membership members of the Transport and General Workers Union in breach of the 'Bridlington Agreement' relating to the 'poaching' of members of another union. The TUC ordered the union to expel the members, and it complied with the TUC ruling. The expulsion was invalid, as the union's rules did not provide for expulsion and such a power could not be implied into the rules.

The rules may confer on the union a general power of expulsion, e.g. for acting contrary to the interests of the union; or particular powers of expulsion which specify the circumstances in which the power can be invoked, e.g. failing to pay the union subscriptions.

Acting-contrary to the interests of the union   Such a phrase is ambiguous and the validity of an expulsion on these grounds has been challenged in the courts on numerous occasions. In *Kelly v. NATSOPA*, a union was given the power by its rules to expel a member for 'conduct detrimental to the interests of the union'. A union member was expelled under this rule, as he worked part-time in the day as a porter, in addition to his full-time employment at night as a printer. The union felt that his full-time work would be adversely affected and that fatigue might make him a danger to his fellow workers. It was held that his expulsion was invalid, as his conduct was not considered by the court to be detrimental. In *Evans v. NUPBPW*, an applicant was accepted for membership of a union on condition that he worked as a casual jobbing hand for a firm of printers. After periods of absence the firm gave his job to a non-unionist. Despite being told by the union that he must do the work, he refused to do so. It was held that his expulsion was lawful as he had acted to the union's detriment.

However, the power of expulsion must be exercised in strict compliance with the provisions of the union's rules. In *Bonsor v. Musicians Union*, a union rule provided that a member could be expelled by a branch committee if his subscriptions were twenty-six weeks in arrears. Bonsor, whose subscriptions were fifty-two weeks in arrears, was expelled by his branch secretary. It was held that his expulsion was void as the power of expulsion could only be exercised by the branch committee, and he was awarded damages against the union.

In *Blackall v. National Union of Foundry Workers*, a union member was fined for working overtime, contrary to a union instruction. He refused to pay the fine and his subscription and was expelled for non-payment of his subscription two days before the final date for payment. It was held that the expulsion was two days premature and therefore void.

Where a rule is found to be ambiguous the courts will interpret such a rule in favour of the weaker party, i.e. the union member. In *Lee v. Showmen's Guild of Great Britain*, a member was expelled after a dispute over a pitch at Bradford fair. He was fined for indulging 'in unfair competition' under the rules of the Guild and was expelled when he refused to pay the fine. It was held that as the Guild had misconstrued the meaning of the term 'unfair competition', Lee's expulsion was void.

Every trade union member who is employed by or seeks employment with an employer where a union membership agreement (closed shop) is in operation, has the right not to be unreasonably expelled from the trade union specified in the union membership agreement (EA 1980 section 4).

Remedies for wrongful expulsion
As an action for wrongful expulsion is technically an action for breach of contract, an expelled member may seek the appropriate remedy from the courts.

(*a*) *Injunction*   A member may seek an injunction ordering union officials not to proceed with the wrongful expulsion, or not to bar his re-instatement as may be the case.

(*b*) *Damages*   A member may seek damages, in addition to the other remedies, to compensate him for any loss sustained as a result of wrongful expulsion. In *Edwards v. SOGAT*, a printer worked for a firm which operated a 'closed shop' and had a 'check off' arrangement with SOGAT. Due to an administrative error the union failed to arrange that his subscription was deducted from his wages, as had been agreed between Edwards and his employer. He fell into arrears, and under a rule which provided that he should automatically cease to be a member if his subscriptions were six weeks in arrear, he ceased to be a member and was dismissed by his employer. SOGAT conceded that he had been wrongly expelled and he was awarded damages of £3500 (1971).

(*c*) *Declaration*   A declaration declares the position of the parties in law. Although it is of moral value only, it is nevertheless observed by the parties. In *Silvester v. National Union of Printers*, a union fined a member for refusing to work overtime. He refused to pay the fine and was subsequently expelled. He obtained a declaration from the courts that the union had misconstructed its own rules, and that his expulsion was *ultra vires* and void.

A member who is unreasonably expelled from a union, or a person who is unreasonably refused membership of a union, where employment is conditional on membership of that union (a closed shop), may make a complaint to a tribunal within six months of the date of expulsion or refusal of membership. An appeal may be made on a question of law or fact to the Employment Appeal Tribunal.

If a tribunal finds the complaint to be well-founded, it must make a declaration to that effect, and may also make an award of compensation. The amount of compensation is 'such as the tribunal considers appropriate for the purpose of compensating the applicant for the loss sustained by him in consequence of the refusal or expulsion which was the subject of the complaint'. The maximum award is thirty weeks pay, plus the maximum compensatory award for unfair dismissal (£11 850). If the union refuses to abide by the tribunal's decision, the complainant may seek redress from the

Employment Appeal Tribunal, which may make an award of up to a maximum of fifty-two weeks pay plus the maximum award of an industrial tribunal (£19 390).

Inter-union disputes

The Trade Union Congress (TUC) at its conference in Bridlington in 1939 drew up a series of rules, known as the Bridlington Agreement, to deal with inter-union disputes. These were amended and extended in 1969 by the Croydon recommendations. In particular these rules deal with the poaching by one union of the members of another union and the extension of a union's sphere of influence. A union must not accept a member of another union whose contributions are outstanding, or who is 'under discipline or penalty'. Neither may a union commence organising activities at any 'establishment or undertaking in respect of any grade of workers in which another union has the majority of workers employed and negotiates wages and conditions unless by arrangement with that union'.

As a result of *Spring v. National Amalgamated Stevedores and Dockers Society*, the TUC drew up a model rule designed to overrule the decision, and enabling a union to expel a member in order to comply with a TUC ruling. It invited all affiliated unions to incorporate this model rule in their rule books.

The effect of one of these rules was considered in *Rothwell v. APEX*. APEX had affected a merger under the Trade Union (Amalgamation) Act 1964 with a staff association (SAGA) in the insurance industry. Another union ASTMS objected to the merger and the TUC Disputes Committee upheld the objection on the grounds that APEX had recruited the members of the smaller union from the area where ASTMS was the appropriate union. In consequence of this ruling, APEX expelled all those members of SAGA who had joined it as a result of the merger. It was held that the expulsion was invalid, as ASTMS had never had anything near to fifty per cent membership of the company concerned (as required by the Bridlington Agreement). The decision of the disputes committee was therefore *ultra vires* and void. It was also unlawful for the union to attempt to undo a merger which had been properly carried out according to statute.

The decision in *Cheall v. APEX* also upholds the TUC disputes machinery. APEX admitted to membership a member of ACTSS without making inquiries of his former union. ACTSS complained to the disputes committee which ordered APEX to terminate the plaintiff's membership. When APEX complied, the plaintiff brought an action for wrongful expulsion. It was held that his expulsion was valid and was not contrary to the rules of natural justice, as the parties to the dispute were unions. The House of Lords also held that the Bridlington Agreement was not contrary to public policy.

An employer who is caught in the middle of an inter-union dispute may seek the assistance of ACAS.

The political fund

The majority of trade unions engage in political activities and set aside funds to further these activities. The Trade Union Act 1913 stipulates that payments for political purposes can only be made from the union's political fund, which must be kept separate from the general fund. A majority of the membership must approve the establishment of a political fund. Any member who does not wish to contribute to the fund must be free to contract out, and must not be placed at any disadvantage if he does so, other then in relation to the control or management of the political fund. However a non-contributor may hold office partly concerned with the management of the political fund. In *Birch v. NUR*, the rules of the union provided that a non-contributor should be 'ineligible to occupy any office or representative position involving any such control or management'. The plaintiff was elected a branch chairman, but the union's national executive declared his election invalid as the union's political fund was controlled by a committee of all branch chairmen. It was held that the national executive's actions amounted to unlawful discrimination, as the plaintiff's office was only partly concerned with the management of the fund.

Members must be informed of their right not to contribute and those members who do not wish to contribute may give written notice in the following form:

Name of Trade Union

I hereby give notice that I object to contribute to the Political Fund of the .... [*Trade Union*], and I am in consequence exempt in manner provided by the Trade Union Act 1913, from contributing to that fund.

A.B.

Address ....

.... day of 1984

An individual cannot give advance notice of his intention to contract out, on becoming a member. He must be a member before he can give notice to contract out. A political fund may be used for the following purposes:

1   The payment of any expenses incurred by a candidate (or prospective candidate) or election to Parliament or other public office
2   The holding of meetings or the distribution of literature in support of any such candidate.
3   The maintenance of any MP or person holding public office.
4   The registration of electors or the selection of any such candidate.
5   The holding of political meetings and the distribution of election literature.

Union secret ballots

Section 1 of the Employment Act 1980 enables the Secretary of State to establish a scheme providing for payments towards expenditure incurred by independent trade unions in holding secret ballots.

The purposes for which a ballot may be held are:

1   Calling or ending a strike or other industrial action;
2   Carrying out an election provided for by the rules of a trade union;
3   Electing a worker who is a member of a trade union to be a representative of other members also employed by his employer;
4   Amending the rules of the union;

5 Obtaining a decision on a resolution to approve a transfer or an amalgamation;
6 Accepting or rejecting an employer's proposal relating to remuneration, hours of work, level of performance, holidays or pensions.

At present the scheme covers postal ballots only. Payments may be made towards the postal costs of a ballot, the stationery and printing costs of the voting papers together with any explanatory literature enclosed with the voting papers.

Section 2 of the Act obliges an employer of more than twenty workers to comply with a request of an independent trade union to permit his premises to be used by employees who are members of that union to vote in a secret ballot. The question on the ballot must relate to any of the above purposes.

13

The Law Relating to Industrial Action

Virtually every form of industrial action involves, at common law, the commission of a tort or a breach of contract, e.g. an employee who goes on strike is invariably in breach of his contract of employment. The freedom to take industrial action, without incurring any liability in tort, is strictly limited to those acts which are done 'in contemplation or furtherance of a trade dispute'.

Trade dispute

A *trade dispute* is defined by section 29 of TULRA (as amended by the EA 1982) as a dispute between workers and their employers which relates wholly or mainly to one or more of the following:

1   Terms and conditions of employment, or the physical conditions in which any workers are required to work;
2   The engagement or non-engagement or termination or suspension of employment or the duties of employment, of one or more workers;
3   The allocation of work or the duties of employment between workers or groups of workers;
4   Matters of discipline;
5   Membership or non-membership of a trade union on the part of a worker;
6   Facilities for officials of trade unions;
7   Machinery for negotiation or consultation, and other matters relating to the foregoing matters including the recognition by

employers or employers' associations of the right of a trade union to represent workers in any such negotiations or consultation or in the carrying out of such procedures.

A lawful trade dispute exists only when workers are in dispute with their own employer, and the dispute is wholly or mainly concerned with employment, pay or conditions of work. A dispute which is connected with these matters rather than wholly or mainly concerned with them is excluded from the definition.

A dispute between a trade union and an employer who is not in dispute is not within the definition of the Act, nor is a dispute between trade unions or groups of workers where no employer is involved. Immunity is granted to a trade dispute which relates to matters occurring outside Great Britain only insofar as the terms and conditions of British workers are affected by the outcome of the dispute.

In *Hadmor Productions Ltd v. Hamilton*, ACTT members employed at Thames Television took a decision to black a series of programmes made by a facility company with freelance ACTT members. The facility company was in the process of selling the programmes to Thames Television. It was held that a trade dispute existed in that it arose out of fears amongst the technicians at Thames Television, for job security in a period of high unemployment.

A strike called for political motives, which has no bearing on employment, is not a trade dispute and therefore has no immunity. In *BBC v. Hearn*, the Association of Broadcasting Staff threatened to take action to prevent transmission of the Cup Final to South Africa, as they opposed racial policies in that country. South Africa was one of a number of countries served by satellite transmission and such action would have blacked out transmission to those other countries. As there was no trade dispute, the BBC was granted an injunction to restrain the union from inducing their members to act in breach of their contracts.

In *Express Newspapers v. Keys*, the general secretaries of four print unions instructed their members to withdraw their labour as part of the TUC 'Day of Action' in protest against Government policies. An injunction was granted restraining the unions from inducing their members to act in breach of their contracts, in what was clearly a political strike. The employer was in no position to concede to the demands of those who took part in the industrial action.

A dispute which aims to effect a change in government policy is not necessarily a political dispute. In *Duport Steels v. Sirs*, the union's primary purpose was to persuade the government, as the paymaster of a nationalised industry, to provide the additional funds to meet a wage claim. This motive did not invalidate the dispute.

'In contemplation of'

Lord Loreburn stated in *Conway v. Wade* that 'either a dispute is imminent and the act is done in expectation of and with a view to it, or that the dispute is already existing and the act is done in support of one side to it'.

In *Bents Brewery Co. Ltd v. Hogan*, a trade union official asked the managers of public houses to disclose information relating to sales and income in these public houses. It was held that the union official was inducing a breach of contract (i.e. disclosure of confidential information by an employee), for although his intention was to obtain information which would help in formulating a claim, there was no dispute in contemplation at that particular time.

A wider interpretation was given to the phrase in 1980 in *Health Computing Ltd v. Meek*. A private company supplying computer systems sought an injunction against NALGO which had instructed its members in the National Health Service not to cooperate with independent computer contractors. NALGO successfully contended that a dispute was contemplated as likely to arise, even though the union had made no demand to management.

'In furtherance of'

The test as to whether an act is 'in furtherance' of a trade dispute is subjective. Immunity will be given if the person who does the act honestly believes at the time he does it that it may help his side to the trade dispute achieve its objectives and he does it for that reason (*Duport Steel Ltd v. Sirs*; *Express Newspapers Ltd v. McShane*).

The act in question must further a trade dispute. An act which is motivated by other considerations may not be regarded as relating to a trade dispute.

In *Torquay Hotels Ltd v. Cousins*, a union blacked the plaintiff's hotel after the hotel's managing director had criticised the union's conduct in an existing dispute involving another Torquay hotel. It was held that there was no trade dispute, and hence no immunity, as the dispute between the union and the managing director or his company was a personal dispute.

An act which is initially in furtherance of a trade dispute may be outside the protected formula if the character of the act later changes because of other extraneous factors. In *Huntley v. Thornton*, the plaintiff's union called a one-day strike but the plaintiff refused to comply with the union instruction and went to work on that day. The district committee of the union recommended that he be expelled from the union, but the union's executive council declined to take action. Nevertheless the local union officials prevented him from obtaining work locally and hounded him out of any job which he succeeded in obtaining. It was held that the local union officials had committed the tort of conspiracy as their acts had become more and more in the nature of a personal vendetta as the matter progressed.

An act may be too remote from the dispute to be in furtherance of that dispute. In *Beaverbrook Newspapers Ltd v. Keys*, the *Daily Mirror* was not published because of a trade dispute. The Daily Express decided to publish additional copies to cater for the demand in the market. The general secretary of SOGAT instructed his members at the Daily Express not to handle these extra copies, as it would weaken the union's dispute with the Daily Mirror. The Daily Express sought an injunction to restrain the union from inducing their employees to break their contracts. An injunction was granted as the union's action was not in furtherance of a trade dispute, as its action was 'too remote to be protected by statute'.

Secondary action

A trade union in dispute with an employer may take action against other employers, who are not parties to the dispute, in order to exert pressure on the first employer. In *Express Newspapers v. McShane*, the National Union of Journalists was in dispute with provincial newspapers. In order to make the strike more effective, it ordered its members in national newspapers to refuse copy from the

Press Association which supplied stories to newspapers. The *Daily Express*, which was not a party to the dispute, sought an injunction to restrain the NUJ's action. It was held that the union's action was in furtherance of a trade dispute.

The House of Lords re-affirmed the decision in *Express Newspapers v. McShane* later in 1980, in *Duport Steels Ltd v. Sirs*. The ISTC, in the course of a prolonged strike with the British Steel Corporation over a wage dispute, called out its members in privately-owned steel firms in order to make the strike more effective. Although there was no dispute with the private employers, it was held that the ISTC's action was in furtherance of a trade dispute.

The Employment Act 1980 limits the secondary action which may be lawfully taken by a union to that which affects the immediate supplier(s) and customer(s) of the employer, with whom the union is in dispute. Any other form of secondary action will not be protected by section 13 of TULRA.

Secondary action in relation to a trade dispute is defined in section 17 of EA 1980, as when a person induces another to break a contract of employment, or interferes or induces another to interfere with its performance; or threatens that a contract of employment under which he or another is employed will be broken or its performance interfered with, or that he will induce another to break a contract of employment or to interfere with its performance.

Three forms of secondary action are permitted:

1   If the purpose of the action is to prevent or disrupt the supply of goods and services during the dispute between an employer who is a party to the dispute and an employer under a contract of employment to which the secondary action relates (EA 1980 section 17.3). For example, a trade dispute exists between an employer A and a trade union T. T is given immunity if it calls upon employees employed by E (another employer) not to deliver goods to A, or accept goods from A.

2   If the purpose of the action is to prevent or disrupt the supply of goods and services during the dispute between any person and an associated employer of an employer who is a party to the dispute. The goods or services are in substitution for goods or services which but for the dispute would have been supplied to or by the employer who is a party to the dispute (EA 1980 section 17.4). For example,

a trade dispute exists between an employer A and a trade union T. A is unable to obtain goods for employer E, and so requests an associated employer M to supply those goods. T may take action against E or M to disrupt the supply of these goods.

Any two employers are to be treated as associated if one is a company of which the other (directly or indirectly) has control, or if both are companies of which a third person (directly or indirectly) has control (EPCA section 153).

3 Lawful picketing by a worker employed (or last employed) by a party to the dispute, or by a trade union official in lawful attendance at the employee's place of work is permitted, in order to prevent or disrupt the supply of goods or services to or by the employer.

Liability at common law

It is necessary to examine the possible areas of tortious liability which encompass an industrial dispute. The torts in question are:

1 Inducing a breach of contract;
2 Procuring a breach of contract;
3 Conspiracy;
4 Intimidation.

1 Inducing a breach of contract

The tort of inducing a breach of contract occurs when a third party unjustifiably induces a breach of contract between an employer and an employee which results in damage to the party concerned. An early example is *Lumley v. Gye*, when Gye was sued for inducing an opera singer named Joanna Wagner to break her contract with the plaintiff, in order to sing at the defendant's theatre.

In order to succeed in an action the plaintiff must prove: the existence of a contract; a breach of that contract; and that the defendant had knowledge of the contract and had induced the breach. It is therefore not unlawful to induce a person not to enter into employment with a certain employer or to induce an employee to terminate his contract by lawful means, e.g. by giving proper notice.

A union official who calls a strike or who takes a significant part in organising a strike could be liable for inducing a breach of contract (as could the trade union). The inducement may take the form of persuasion, instruction, direction, threat, order or communication. Its effect must be to induce a breach of contract.

Liability may also arise if a trade union official induces an employer to dismiss an employee in breach of contract. This form of pressure may be achieved by threats or otherwise. If an employer dismisses an employee as a result of such pressure, but gives the employee the appropriate notice or wages in lieu of notice, no tort is committed.

In contrast to the direct inducement cited above, a trade union may incur liability when it boycotts or blacks a commercial contract and thereby indirectly induces a breach of contract. In *Torquay Hotels Ltd v. Cousins*, a trade union which was in dispute with the plaintiff's hotel company (after criticism of the union's dispute with other hotels in the area), contacted Esso Ltd's drivers who supplied oil to the plaintiff's and instructed them not to deliver the fuel. An injunction was granted restraining the union from procuring a breach of the contract by Esso Ltd to supply the hotel with oil, by inducing Esso Ltd's employees to breach their contracts of employment.

Defence Section 13.1 of TULRA (as amended) provides a defence to this tort. It states 'An act done by a person in contemplation of furtherance of a trade dispute shall not be actionable in tort on the ground only:

1 That it induces another person to break a contract or interferes or induces any other person to interfere with its performance; or
2 That it consists in his threatening that a contract (whether one to which he is a party or not) will be broken or its performance interfered with, or that he will induce another person to break a contract or interfere with its performance.'

This section gives protection to a person who, in contemplation or furtherance of a trade union dispute, induces or procures a breach of contract. It covers both employment and commercial contracts.

2 Procuring a breach of contract

The tort of procuring a breach of contract occurs when pressure is brought against a contracting party at second-hand. The plaintiff must show that a contract exists; that the defendant induced, persuaded or procured employees to breach their contracts of employment; and that the necessary consequence of the employees' breach of contract is the breach of the contract forming the subject matter of the action.

In *Stratford v. Lindley*, the plaintiff was the chairman of two companies. The holding company employed forty-eight lightermen, of whom forty-five belonged to the Transport and General Workers Union (TGWU) and three to the Watermen's Union (WU). The plaintiff eventually recognised the TGWU for negotiating purposes. The WU, in order to bring pressure on Stratford to make him recognise that union, put an embargo on the barges hired out and repaired by the subsidiary company. As a result the barges were not returned to the company's moorings when the hiring contracts ended, causing a loss to the company of £1000 a week. The WU were liable for indirectly procuring a breach of contract between the company and the hirers, who under the hiring contract were to return the barges to the company's moorings.

Another aspect of the tort is illustrated by *Daily Mirror Newspapers Ltd v. Gardner*, where the publishers of the *Daily Mirror* notified the wholesalers of a price increase in the paper and of a reduction in the discount allowed to wholesalers. The newspaper retailers, whose profit margin depended on the number of copies sold and the wholesalers' discount, attempted to bring pressure to bear on the company by proposing a week's boycott on the sale of the paper. The company obtained an injunction restraining the officials of the newspaper retailers' association from procuring a breach of the contract between the newspaper company and the wholesalers.

Defence Section 13.1 of TULRA (as amended) adopts a similar approach to this tort as it does to the tort of inducing a breach of contract, and affords protection against the tort of procuring breach of a commercial contract.

3 Conspiracy

This tort occurs when two or more persons combine to do an act, which although lawful in itself, causes damage to a third party's trade or interests. There is no conspiracy if the real and predominant purpose of the defendants is to advance their legitimate interests. In *Mogul Steamship Co. v. McGregor, Gow and Co.*, the plaintiff alleged that the defendants, who were an associated body of traders in China tea, had caused him loss by threatening certain merchants in China that unless they ceased to act as his agent, the association's agency would be withdrawn from them. It was held that such action could be justified on the grounds of legitimate self-protection.

Another form of conspiracy exists when two or more persons combine to injure a third party by unlawful means. In *Quinn v. Leatham*, a butcher employed non-union labour. He refused to heed a union's request to dismiss the men, but offered to pay their subscription arrears if they were admitted to the union. The trade union officials refused as they wanted to teach the non-unionists a lesson and make them 'walk the streets for twelve months'. The union then persuaded his chief customer to cease dealing with him by threatening to call a strike of that customer's workmen. The customer did so and it was held that the union was liable for conspiracy as its legitimate activities could have been achieved by accepting Leatham's initial offer.

However, certain forms of collective pressures are permissible and lawful. In *Crofter Hand-Woven Harris Tweed Co. v. Veitch*, the TGWU wished to obtain 100 per cent membership in a company manufacturing Harris Tweed on the Isle of Lewis. It therefore instructed the dockers at the port of Stornaway (who were union members) to cease handling yarn imported by the plaintiff company and the finished cloth manufactured from that yarn. The plaintiff company were importing the yarn at a cheaper price than the yarn spun on the island. It was held that as the TGWU believed in good faith that its actions was in the best interests of the Harris Tweed industry, there was no conspiracy.

The House of Lords thus effectively reversed *Quinn v. Leatham* by recognising that establishing a 'closed shop' was a legitimate trade union activity.

Defence   Section 13.4 of TULRA (as amended) provides a defence to this tort. It states 'An agreement or combination by two or more persons to do or procure the doing of any act in contemplation or furtherance of a trade dispute shall not be actionable in tort if the act is one which, if done without any such agreement or combination would not be actionable in tort.'

This means that an act which is not actionable if done in contemplation or furtherance of a trade dispute by one individual, does not become actionable on the grounds of conspiracy if done by a group of individuals. It is not unlawful for an employee to threaten strike action, and it is not a conspiracy for a group of employees to threaten such action.

4 Intimidation

The tort of intimidation consists of a threat to commit an unlawful act which results in damage to the plaintiff. The case of *Rookes v. Barnard* resurrected this ancient tort in 1964. The Association of Engineering and Shipbuilding Draughtsmen threatened to call a strike at London Airport (in order to preserve an informal closed shop) unless the plaintiff, a non-union member, was dismissed. This action constituted the tort of intimidation. The threat to strike was in breach of contract as a no-strike clause had been incorporated into the contract of every individual employee.

Defence Section 13.1(b) of TULRA (as amended) gives protection against the tort of intimidation. It states 'An act done by a person *in contemplation or furtherance of a trade dispute* shall not be actionable in tort on the ground only that it consists in his threatening that a contract (whether one to which he is a party or not) will be broken or its performance interfered with, or that he will induce another person to break a contract or to interfere with its performance'.

This section gives protection against a threat to break a contract of employment, and against a threat to induce a breach of contract, or to interfere with its performance.

Union membership or recognition requirements in contract

Any term or condition in a contract for the supply of goods or services which requires a person to use only union labour, or non-union labour is void.

It is also unlawful for a person, on the grounds of union membership or non-membership to:

1 Exclude a particular person's name from a list of approved suppliers of goods or services;
2 Terminate a contract for the supply of goods or services;
3 Exclude a particular person from tendering for the supply of goods or services;
4 Fail to permit a particular person to submit a tender; or
5 Otherwise determine not to enter into a contract with a particular person for the supply of goods or services (EA 1982 section 12).

A person who is adversely affected by any of these acts may bring an action in respect of a breach of statutory duty, and so recover damages.

Any term or condition of a contract for the supply of goods or services is void in so far as it purports to require any party to the contract to:

1 Recognise one or more trade unions; or
2 Negotiate or consult with any official of one or more trade unions (EA 1982 section 13).

A breach of this section will entitle an injured party to bring an action for damages.

Section 14 of the EA 1982 provides that any industrial action to induce a person to contravene sections 12 and 13 of the Act (above) is unlawful and is not given the trade dispute immunity of section 13 of TULRA. Section 14 also provides that any industrial action or threat of industrial action which interferes with the supply of goods and services is unlawful if the reason for taking such action is:

(*a*) That work done or to be done in connection with the supply of goods or services has been or is likely to be done by non-union labour or by members of a particular trade union; or
(*b*) The supplier of the goods does not employ union labour, or does not recognise, negotiate or consult with a trade union.

These provisions, designed to protect non-union companies, also protect unionised companies against discrimination as they employ union members.

Trade union immunity

A union's liability in respect of actions for inducing or threatening to induce a breach of contract or for conspiracy, is limited to those acts which are authorised or endorsed by a responsible person.

A responsible person is defined as:

(*a*)   The principal executive committee;
(*b*)   Any other person who is empowered by the union's rules to authorise or endorse such actions;
(*c*)   The president or general secretary;
(*d*)   Any employed official;
(*e*)   Any union committee to whom an employed official regularly reports.

An act will not be taken as having been authorised or endorsed by a responsible person if that person was prevented by the rules from authorising or endorsing the act in question, or if the act was repudiated by the principal executive committee or by the president or general secretary. The repudiation must be made as soon as is reasonably practicable after the purported authorisation or endorsement of the act has come to the knowledge of the principal executive committee, or of the president, or of the general secretary, who must not behave in a manner which is inconsistent with the purported repudiation. The person who purported to authorise or endorse the act must be notified in writing and without delay of its repudiation.

A trade union which is unable to claim immunity for its actions may be sued for an injunction and damages in tort. The amount which may be awarded as damages against a union is limited, and is determined by the size of the union's membership.

The amounts are as follows:

£10 000 if the membership is less then 5000
£50 000 if the membership exceeds 5000 but is less than 25 000
£125 000 if the membership exceeds 25 000 but is less than 100 000
£250 000 if the membership exceeds 100 000.

Any damages, costs or expenses awarded in an action against a trade union cannot be recovered from protected property of the union. Protected property is defined as:

1　Property belonging to the trustees, other than in their capacity as trustees;
2　Property belonging to any member, other than property owned jointly with other members;
3　Property belonging to any union official;
4　Property comprised in a political fund or a provident benefit fund.

Strikes

An employee who takes strike action withdraws his labour and is therefore in breach of his contract of employment. An employer may, if he so wishes, treat the contract as terminated.

In *Simmons v. Hoover Ltd*, an employee on strike was dismissed by his employer. It was held that although the real reason for the dismissal was redundancy, the employee was not entitled to a redundancy payment as he had repudiated his contract of employment by taking strike action.

Most employers regard a strike as a suspension of the contract. Many factors dictate this course of action, e.g. industrial relations, the cost of training a new work force.

This view is also taken by the legislature, as strike action is not regarded as breaking continuity of employment in calculating an employee's length of service when claiming a redundancy payment, compensation for unfair dismissal, or entitlement to maternity leave and pay. The period during which an employee was on strike is subtracted from his total length of service.

An employee who takes strike action without giving his employer adequate notice of his intentions runs a risk of being sued by his employer for damages for breach of contract. In *Ebbw Vale Steel, Iron & Co. v. Tew*, the defendent was held liable in damages for refusing to work a shift in a mine. The measure of the damages was the value of the coal he would have dug, less the expenses incurred in obtaining it. (see also *NCB v. Galley*)

The view held by the Donovan Commission was that an employee who gives notice of strike action cannot be regarded as acting in breach of contract, as he has terminated his employment by giving notice to his employer. The employer may nevertheless treat the contract as terminated.

An employer has several options open to him in these circumstances. He may, as most employers do, ignore the legal implications and treat the contract as subsisting, or he may re-instate or re-engage the employee. An employee who is re-instated will be treated as if his employment after the strike ran on without a break from his employment prior to the strike. An employee who is re-engaged will begin a new period of employment from the time he commences work.

An employee who takes strike action, despite having entered into a no-strike agreement (i.e. until an agreed disputes procedure has been followed), is acting in breach of contract, and may not only be dismissed, but also sued for damages for breach of contract. The measure of damages recoverable will be the loss actually suffered by the employer.

Industrial action short of strike action may nevertheless amount to a repudiation of the contract. A work-to-rule (*Secretary of State for Employment v. ASLEF*), or a refusal to deliver goods to a destination 'blacked' by the union, amounts to a breach of the contract and its repudiation by an employee. Notice by an employee that he intends such action is an anticipatory breach of the contract and an employer is entitled to sue for breach of contract on receipt of such notice. The employer can treat the contract as repudiated when the employee's action commences.

Picketing

It is lawful for a person in contemplation or furtherance of a trade dispute to attend:

(*a*) At or near his own place of work; or
(*b*) If he is a trade union official, at or near the place of work of a member of that union whom he is accompanying and whom he represents, for the purpose *only* of peacefully obtaining or communicating information, or peacefully persuading any persons to work or abstain from working.

If a person works or normally works at more than one place, or at a place where it is impracticable to picket, his place of work will be any of his employer's premises from which he works, or from which his work is administered. A worker whose employment is terminated in connection with a trade dispute is permitted to picket at his former place of work.

A trade union official who has been elected or appointed to represent some members of the union will be regarded as representing only those members. Otherwise a trade union official will be regarded as representing all its members.

Any other form of picketing may render a picket liable to civil or criminal liability.

Civil liability

A picket may be liable for the tort of private nuisance, where he interferes with another's use or enjoyment of land, e.g. blocking an access; or for the tort of trespass to the highway if he uses the highway for any other purpose 'otherwise than reasonably for passage and repassage and . . . any other purpose reasonably incidental thereto' (*Hickman v. Maisey*).

Criminal liability

A picket may commit any of the following offences:

(*a*) *Obstructing the highway*   An offence is committed if a person without lawful authority or excuse wilfully obstructs free passage along the highway (Highways Act 1959 section 121).

In *Broome v. DPP*, a trade union official having failed to persuade a lorry driver not to deliver goods to a factory where a dispute was in progress, stood in front of the lorry to prevent its progress. He was told by a policeman to move, but refused and was later convicted of obstructing the highway.

(*b*) *Breach of the peace*   A picket may be found guilty of a breach of the peace if he obstructs a police constable in the execution of his duty. In *Piddington v. Bates*, several pickets arrived outside a factory where a dispute was in progress. Two pickets were stationed at the front gate, and four at the back gate. A police constable asked two of the pickets on the back gate to leave, as he reasonably apprehended a breach of the peace, and they did so. One returned and tried to rejoin the picket line, pushing past the constable, and was arrested. It was held that a policeman may 'take such steps as he thinks proper', and that this includes limiting the number of pickets.

(c) *Unlawful assembly*   This offence is committed when three or more persons gather together for the purpose of committing or preparing to commit a crime involving the use of violence, or in order to carry out a lawful or unlawful purpose in an unlawful way. In *R. v. Jones* (the Shrewsbury picket case), there was evidence of threats of violence against self-employed blacklegs, and as a result two flying pickets were gaoled for substantial terms.

(d) *The Conspiracy and Protection of Property Act 1875*   Section 7 provides that a criminal offence is committed if a person wilfully and without legal authority:

1 Uses violence to or intimidates another person, his wife or children or injures his property;
2 Persistently follows that person from place to place;
3 Hides any tools, clothes or other property of such person, or deprives him of their use or hinders their use;
4 Watches or besets any house where that person resides, or the approach to such house;
5 Follows that person in the street with two or more persons in a disorderly manner.

(e) *Public nuisance*   A picket may be guilty of a public nuisance if he obstructs the highway and prevents the public from exercising their lawful right of free passage.

In *Tynan v. Balmer*, the leader of a strike led forty pickets in an orderly manner in a circle on the road in front of the factory's main gate and effectively prevented traffic from entering the factory. He was asked by a police constable to stop the pickets from circling, and on refusing to do so was arrested. It was held that there was an obstruction of the highway and the pickets had committed a public nuisance.

A picket has no right to stop vehicles. He may persuade a driver to stop, but he has no right to make him stop and listen (*Broome v. DPP*).

'One is familiar with persons at the side of the road signalling to a driver requesting him to stop. It is then for the driver to decide whether he will stop or not. That, in my view, a picket is entitled to do. If the driver stops, the picket can talk to him, but only for as long as the driver is willing to listen.' (per Lord Reid in *Broome v. DPP*).

The *Code of Practice on Picketing* suggests that in general the number of pickets should not exceed six at any entrance to any work place. Frequently a smaller number would be appropriate. It regards mass picketing as non-productive in that it is not an attempt at peaceful persuasion, but constitutes obstruction, and possibly intimidation.

Secondary picketing

Secondary picketing, i.e. picketing other than at one's place of work is, with limited exceptions, unlawful. Such a picket is generally liable in tort for the consequences of his actions, e.g. he can be sued in tort if he induces workers to break their contracts of employment.

Two forms of secondary picketing are permitted:

1 Picketing an immediate customer or supplier of the employer in the dispute with the aim of disrupting services to and from the employer;
2 Picketing an associated employer of the employer in the dispute with the aim of preventing substitute supplies of goods or services which would in normal circumstances have been provided to or by the employer in dispute.

14

Sickness and Unemployment Benefit; Industrial Injuries

The Social Security Act 1975 is a consolidating statute which combines the national insurance scheme with the industrial injuries scheme. The national insurance scheme provides a variety of benefits for those who are unemployed, and for those who are unable to work because of sickness or illness; while the industrial injuries scheme provides benefits for an employee who is injured at work. Both schemes are contributory in that they are financed out of a fund which consists largely of national insurance contributions.

Sickness benefit

Under the provisions of the Social Security and Housing Benefits Act 1982, sickness benefit is payable initially by the employer in the form of statutory sick pay, followed by state sickness benefit for those employees who have paid sufficient national insurance contributions.

Statutory sick pay

An employee is entitled to eight weeks statutory sick pay from his employer in any tax year. He will not be entitled to claim state sickness benefit until he has exhausted his entitlement to statutory sick pay (SSP).

An employer may recoup the gross amount of any payment of SSP by withholding the amount from the monthly national insurance contributions sent to the Inland Revenue or from the monthly tax return. Basically, all employees are covered by the scheme if they are absent because of personal sickness for four or more days in a row.

An employee is entitled to SSP if his *day of incapacity* for work forms part of the *period of incapacity* for work; falls within the *period of entitlement*; and counts as a *qualifying day*.

These terms are interpreted as follows:

Day of incapacity   A day when he is incapable because of a specific disease or disablement of doing work he might reasonably be expected to do.

Period of incapacity   A period of four or more consecutive days of sickness.

Period of entitlement   This starts with the first day of incapacity and ends when the period of incapacity has ended, or when the contract of employment is terminated, or when entitlement to SSP has been exhausted, or when a woman who is pregnant is disqualified under the terms of the Act.

A qualifying day will usually be regarded as a day on which an employee would have been available for work, had he not been sick. An employer and employee should agree on any pattern of qualifying days as long as there is at least one in each week. An employee is not entitled to SSP until he has been off sick for at least three qualifying days (called *waiting days*). Any qualifying day during a four-day spell of sickness can count as a waiting day.

Two or more periods of incapacity for work which are separated by fourteen calendar days or less are regarded as linked, and count as one period of incapacity. If an employee who has three qualifying days in one period of incapacity and then has a second linked spell, he will be entitled to payment of SSP from the first qualifying day in the second spell.

There are three different rates of SSP. The amount payable depends on the employee's average earnings in the eight weeks before his absence due to sickness.

Rate (£)	Earnings per week (£)
42.25	68 or more
35.45	48.50 → 67.99
28.58	in any other case

Certain employees are excluded from entitlement to SSP:

(*a*) An employee who is incapacitated from work for less than four days;

(*b*) An employee who is over minimum State pension age (65 male, 60 female) on the first day of sickness;

(*c*) An employee who is employed under a contract of employment for three months or less;

(*d*) An employee whose average weekly earnings is less than the lower earnings limit for paying national insurance contributions – at present less than £32.50 a week;

(*e*) An employee who goes sick within fifty-seven days of a previous claim for one of the following State benefits: sickness benefit, invalidity pension, maternity allowance, or unemployment benefit (in limited circumstances);

(*f*) An employee who goes sick during a stoppage of work at his place of employment due to a trade dispute, unless he can prove that he has not taken part in the trade dispute and has no direct interest in it;

(*g*) A pregnant woman who is off sick in the time starting eleven weeks before her expected week of confinement and ending six weeks after;

(*h*) An employee who has already received eight weeks SSP from an employer in a current tax year or in one spell of sickness;

(*i*) An employee who is sick while abroad outside the European Community;

(*j*) An employee who is in legal custody;

(*k*) An employee who has not commenced work under a contract of service.

State sickness benefit and unemployment benefit

A claimant will only be entitled to either of these benefits if he satisfies the contribution conditions relating to that benefit, and if he belongs to the class of persons entitled to that particular benefit.

Contributions to the National Insurance Fund from insured persons and employers are divided into four categories.

Class One Primary contributions are paid by employed earners, while secondary contributions are paid by employers. Both primary and secondary contributions are earnings-related.

Class Two   Flat rate contributions paid by the self-employed.
Class Three   Voluntary flat rate contributions paid by contributors to secure extra benefits or make up previous deficiencies.
Class Four   Contributions levied on the basis of annual Schedule D returns, i.e. on the basis of profits or gains arising from any trade, business, profession, office or vocation. There is no entitlement to any benefit.

Unemployment benefit is only payable in respect of Class 1 contributions, while both Class 1 and 2 contributors are entitled to sickness benefit.

The contribution conditions which must usually be satisfied for both these benefits are that the claimant:

(*a*)   Must have actually paid contributions of the relevant class, on earnings of at least twenty-five times the weekly lower earnings limit in any one tax year since 1975; and
(*b*)   Must have paid or been credited with contributions of the relevant class of at least fifty times the weekly lower earnings limit in the tax year on which the claim is based.

If the first condition is satisfied, but not the second, benefit may be payable at a reduced rate.

Neither sickness nor unemployment benefit is normally payable for the first three days absence from work. There are limited exceptions in the case of sickness benefit.

A claimant is entitled to benefit in respect of any day of unemployment forming part of a period of interruption of employment, which is made up of:

(*a*)   At least two days unemployment (whether consecutive or not) in any six consecutive days (excluding Sundays); or
(*b*)   At least four consecutive days (excluding Sundays) of incapacity for work.

Any periods of interruption of employment, not separated by more than eight weeks, are regarded as one period of interruption of employment.

The claimant must show that he is capable of work, and also available for work to be entitled to unemployment benefit. It is payable for up to a year in any period of interruption of employment. After this time the claimant must requalify for benefit by working for at least sixteen hours a week for a minimum period of thirteen weeks.

Sickness benefit is payable for a maximum period of 168 days (when it may be replaced by invalidity benefit). This includes days when a claimant was paid maternity allowance, and days when there was an entitlement to sickness benefit but injury benefit was paid instead. It is not payable for an absence from work of less than four consecutive days.

A claimant who is not incapable of work may nevertheless be deemed to be incapable of work and therefore entitled to benefit, in the following circumstances:

(*a*)   If he is suffering from some specific disease or bodily or mental disablement, provided that:
   (i)   he is under medical care in respect of such a disease or disablement; and
   (ii) it is certified by a registered medical practitioner that by reason of such disease or disablement he should abstain from work, and
   (iii) he does not work.

(*b*)   He is excluded from work on the certificate of a Medical Officer for Environmental Health, and is under medical observation by reason of his being a carrier or having been in contact with a case of infectious disease.

Disqualification from sickness benefit
A claimant may be disqualified from receiving sickness benefit for a period of up to six weeks if:

(*a*)   1He has become incapable of work through his own misconduct; or
(*b*)   He fails without good cause to attend for, or to submit himself to such medical or other examination or treatment as may be required or to observe any prescribed rules of behaviour.

There is only one reported decision relating to disqualification for misconduct and this implies that the misconduct must be wilful. In that case the incapacity was due to alcoholism. It was for the claimant to show that his will-power had been so impaired by his addiction to drink that he was unable to moderate his drinking habits. A claimant will not be disqualified if the incapacity is due to pregnancy or venereal disease.

A claimant will be disqualified under (*b*) if he fails, without good cause, to attend for examination or treatment. If a claimant is ill, or has a physical disability which prevents him from attending an examination, this will constitute good cause. A claimant (a Christian Scientist) who objected on the grounds that her religious beliefs did not permit treatment or medical examination was not disqualified from benefit.

A claimant will not usually be disqualified if he fails to attend for or to submit to vaccination or innoculation of any kind, or to undergo a surgical operation. A refusal to submit to a minor operation may well be regarded as unreasonable conduct.

A claimant will be disqualified if he fails, without good cause, to observe any of the following rules of behaviour:

(*a*) To refrain from behaviour calculated to retard his recovery, and to answer any reasonable enquiries to ascertain whether he is doing so;

(*b*) Not to be absent from his place of residence without leaving word where he may be found;

(*c*) Not to do any work for which remuneration is, or would ordinarily be payable.

Disqualification from unemployment benefit

A claimant will not be entitled to unemployment benefit in the following circumstances:

1   If he loses his employment as a result of a stoppage of work due to a trade dispute at his place of employment. He will be disqualified from receiving benefit for as long as the stoppage continues, unless he can show that he is not participating or has any direct interest in the dispute. A trade dispute is defined as 'any dispute between employers and employees, which is connected with the employment or non-employment or the terms of employment or the conditions of employment of any persons, whether employees in the employment of the employer with whom the dispute arises, or not'. (SSA section 19)

A claimant may seek to prove that he is not participating in the trade dispute. Participating is given a very wide meaning, and involves some degree of active support for one of the parties. It has been held that attendance at a meeting called to find a solution to a dispute is participation in the dispute. An employee who does not cross the picket line is participating in a trade dispute, as is an employee who is prevented by force from crossing the picket line. In the latter situation there is an extension of the main dispute to include the dispute between the employee and the pickets.

A claimant is regarded as directly interested if the settlement of the dispute has an immediate effect on his remuneration or conditions of work. A surface worker laid off as a result of a dispute at a mine, relating to bonus payments, was held to have a direct interest as the question of bonus payments affected every person employed at the mine. In contrast, a paint line operator, at a car factory, laid off as a result of a pay dispute of assembly line workers had no direct interest in the dispute. His pay was subject to a separate agreement, and although he had an interest in the outcome of the dispute in so far as it related to his future pay, it was not a direct interest.

An employee whose employment is indefinitely suspended within twelve working days of a stoppage of work at the employee's place of work must *prima facie* be presumed to have lost his employment as a result of the stoppage. This presumption may be rebutted by the claimant, who may provide evidence to prove otherwise.

2   A claimant may also be disqualified from receiving unemployment benefit for up to six weeks, in the following circumstances:

(*a*) Where he has lost his employment through his misconduct, or has voluntarily left such employment without just cause;

(*b*) Where after a situation in any suitable employment has been properly notified to him as vacant or about to become vacant, he has without good cause refused or failed to apply for that situation or refused to accept that situation when offered to him;

(*c*) Where he has neglected to avail himself of reasonable opportunities of suitable employment;

(*d*) Where he has without good cause refused or failed to carry out any official recommendations given to him with a view to assisting him to find suitable employment. The recommendations must be reasonable having regard to his circumstances and to the means of obtaining that employment usually adopted in the district in which he resides, or

(*e*) Where he has without good cause refused or failed to avail himself of a reasonable opportunity of receiving training approved by the Secretary of State in his case for the purpose of becoming or keeping fit for entry into, or return to, regular employment.

The purpose of these restrictions is to discourage voluntary unemployment.

If misconduct is alleged, it must be an act or omission which is related to the employment. It includes 'industrial shortcomings, disobedience, faulty workmanship, idleness, unauthorised absence, some types of carelessness, and conduct . . . connected with the employment' which adversely affects the claimant's proper discharge of his duties (R. J. A. Temple, Chief Commissioner).

A bus driver who lost his licence as a result of a motoring offence, committed while on holiday, was held to be disqualified from benefit due to his misconduct. A manager of a pharmacy was dismissed when a shortage of cash was discovered at his place of work. Although subsequently acquitted of embezzlement in criminal proceedings, he was nevertheless disqualified from benefit on the grounds that his carelessness and inefficiency amounted to misconduct.

A claimant will usually be regarded as having voluntarily left employment without just cause if, dissatisfied with certain matters connected with his employment, he leaves without recourse to established grievance and disciplinary procedures, where these are in existence. A similar presumption will arise if, as a trade union member, he leaves his employment for similar reasons without seeking his union's assistance in settling the matters in dispute.

A woman who refused to undergo an X-ray examination as a prerequisite of employment as a canteen assistant was disqualified as she had left her employment voluntarily without just cause. There are situations where a claimant will be regarded as having a justifiable reason for leaving his employment, e.g. a reduction in wages, pressing social or domestic personal circumstances, difficulty in travelling to work, or an employer not complying with the terms of the contract of employment.

There are four grounds, namely (b) (c) (d) and (e) above,

under which a claimant is disqualified if he unreasonably refuses a suitable opportunity of employment. A claimant who attended an interview for work as a parcel porter, in a dirty and unshaven state, was held to be disqualified from benefit. An unmarried labourer in the Shetland Islands, who had been unemployed for seven months, was disqualified from benefit when he unreasonably refused an offer of employment in the south of England. An electrician sent by his employment exchange for an interview as a maintenance electrician was disqualified from benefit as he had refused to complete an application form for the post. He had failed to apply for the post and was not able to show that the work was unsuitable.

Section 20 of the SSA gives guidance as to what may be considered suitable employment. It provides that certain employment will not be regarded as suitable if it is:

(a) Employment in a situation vacant in consequence of a stoppage of work due to a trade dispute; or

(b) Employment in the claimant's usual occupation in the district where he was last ordinarily employed, but at a lower rate of pay, or less favourable conditions than those which he might reasonably have expected to obtain had he not become unemployed; or

(c) Employment in the claimant's usual occupation in any other district at a lower rate of pay or on less favourable conditions than those generally observed in the district by agreement between employers' and employees' associations or by good employers.

These provisions prevent an unemployed person from being compelled to act as a strike breaker or having to accept employment at substandard wages.

After a reasonable time has elapsed, employment will not be regarded as unsuitable, by reason only that it is not the claimant's usual occupation. The pay and conditions of employment offered in that other occupation must be as favourable as those generally observed by agreement between employers' and employees' associations, or provided by a good employer for that type of employment.

Industrial injuries

To qualify for industrial injuries or disablement benefit the claimant must be an employed earner i.e. he or she must be gainfully employed under a contract of service, or in an office whose emoluments are taxed under Schedule E of the Income and Corporation Taxes Act 1970.

It may be paid after a period of ninety days has elapsed since the date of the accident or ninety days from the first day when the claimant was disabled by the disease (whether or not he has been off work during this time). An employee who has suffered an industrial injury may claim statutory sick pay and sickness benefit prior to the expiration of the ninety days. If he is not entitled to SSP he may nevertheless claim state sickness benefit from the date of the accident on the basis of incapacity. (In these circumstances the benefit is not contribution-based.)

The claimant must show that he has suffered 'personal injury caused by accident arising out of and in the course of his (her) employment' or that he is suffering from a prescribed disease.

Personal injury caused by accident

A personal injury is an 'injury to the living body of a human being' and covers 'hurt to body or mind'. A person suffering from nervous shock or nervous disorder caused by an accident is entitled to benefit in these circumstances. In *Yates v. South Kirkby Colliery Ltd*, a miner tended a fellow worker who later died of his injuries following a colliery explosion. The miner suffered nervous shock. It was held to be a personal injury as 'nervous shock due to accident which causes incapacity is as much personal injury by accident as a broken leg'.

An accident has been defined as 'an unlooked-for mishap or an untoward event which is not expected or designed'. It is this and very much more, and includes the unlawful act of a third party.

In *Trim Joint District School v. Kelly*, the mother of a schoolmaster, killed by pupils whom he threatened to punish, was entitled to benefit as he was killed as a result of an accident. An employee who called for her employer and was scalded by boiling water thrown by her employer's daughter-in-law was also held to have suffered an accident arising out of her employment.

A wide range of incidents have been held to qualify as 'accidents', including being struck by disintegrating machinery; contracting pneumonia as a result of working in water; a rupture caused by over-exertion in turning a wheel; being attacked and robbed while collecting insurance premiums; and contracting anthrax by being infected by a bacillus, when sorting wool (*Brintons v. Turvey*).

An accident must be distinguished from a process, which does not entitle the claimant to benefit. A process is regarded as a physiological change which occurs over a period of time, e.g. a straining of chest muscles caused by lifting weights daily, and a doctor who contracted tuberculosis over a period of time (as opposed to penetration of the lung on a single occasion).

However, a psycho-neurotic condition, caused by a machine producing explosive reports at intermittent intervals was not regarded as a process, but as a 'series of accidents'. The intervals between each report were irregular and infrequent and were therefore incapable of forming a continuous process.

Arising out of and in the course of employment

An accident which occurs in the course of the claimant's employment is deemed, in the absence of evidence to the contrary, to have arisen out of that employment. The employment must therefore be the cause of the accident, e.g. An employee who suffers a heart attack whilst working will be unable to claim benefit under this heading, unless he can show that his heart attack resulted from his work.

It must be shown that the risks of employment are greater than, or different from, those encountered by members of the public, e.g. a coal miner struck by a car when crossing a main road to reach the pit head baths was held to be subject to the same risks as a member of the public. Similarly, a baker who suffered frost-bite when driving his cart in frosty weather was held to be no more exposed to frost-bite than anyone else working in the open. However, a police motor cyclist who suffered an eye injury in the course of his employment was held entitled to benefit as he was subject to greater risks by the nature of his job than an ordinary member of the public.

For an accident to arise in the course of employment, the claimant must prove that the accident occurred at his normal place of work during his normal hours of work, when he was carrying out his normal activity. As the place of work and the hours of work and the nature of the work of the majority of employees are generally fixed, they will have little difficulty in satisfying these conditions. There is a presumption that every accident arises out of in the course of employment, and the insurance officer must prove otherwise in order to rebut this presumption.

In *Thom v. Sinclair*, a female worker was injured when a wall of an adjoining property collapsed on the shed where she was working. This caused the roof to cave in and she was injured. As she was obliged to be in the shed, the accident had arisen in the course of her employment.

An employee will normally be in the course of his employment once he arrives at his employer's premises, and will remain so until he leaves the premises. This also extends to access to the premises, as long as the public do not have a similar right of access. An employee injured when cycling to work on a road owned by his employers was held to be in the course of employment. An employee who arrived at work early and changed into uniform before visiting the canteen for a cup of coffee was also held to be in the course of employment, even though she had not clocked on for work.

Examples of activities which have been held to be reasonably incidental to employment include: having a meal on the premises, working overtime, having a bath after duty in a mine, and attending a union meeting during a lunch break to deal with matters relating to the employment.

An accident which occurs when an employee takes steps at his place of work 'to rescue succour or protect persons who are, or are thought to be or possibly to be injured or imperilled, or to avert or minimise serious damage to property' is deemed to arise out of and in the course of his employment (SSA section 54).

Employees who suffer an accident whilst travelling from one place of work to another are entitled to injury benefit, as are employees whose work involves constant travelling, e.g. sales representatives, journalists, or home helps. The employment of the latter group of employees does not commence (for the purposes of the SSA) until their arrival at the first call of the day.

An employee who has to work away from home, and who is required by his employer to stay at specified accommodation is entitled to injury benefit if he suffers an accident while going to or from that accommodation. If an employee has a choice of accommodation, and an accident occurs in those circumstances, such an accident is regarded as being outside the scope of the SSA.

An employee who travels to and from work on services used by members of the public will not be entitled to injury benefit if an accident occurs in the course of such a journey. If, however, he is travelling as a passenger in any vehicle, with the express or implied permission of his employer, any accident which occurs in the course of that journey will be deemed to arise out of and in the course of his employment if 'at the time of the accident, the vehicle (i) is being operated by or on behalf of his employer or some other person by whom it is provided in pursuance of arrangements made with his employer; and (ii) is not being operated in the ordinary course of a public transport service'. (SSA, section 53).

A *vehicle* includes a ship, vessel, aircraft or hovercraft. The accident must occur while the claimant is a passenger, so that an accident which takes place when walking to meet the vehicle or when transferring from one vehicle to another is not covered by the Act.

Various miscellaneous situations are dealt with in section 55, which provides that 'an accident shall be treated . . . as arising out of an employed earner's employment if:

(*a*) The accident arises in the course of the employment; and
(*b*) The accident either is caused by another person's misconduct, skylarking or negligence, or by steps taken in consequence of any such misconduct, skylarking or negligence, or by the behaviour or presence of an animal (including a bird, fish or insect), or is caused by or consists of the employed earner being struck by any object or by lightning; and
(*c*) The employed earner did not directly or indirectly induce or contribute to the happening of the accident by his conduct outside the employment, or by an act not incidental to the employment.'

Examples of such situations dealt with in (*b*) are: a bus driver who was stung by a wasp; an agricultural worker struck by lightning.

Part (*c*) deals with the 'different risk'. An employer will be disentitled if he creates a different risk by his conduct, and that different risk was the real cause of the accident, e.g. an employee caused an explosion when, in attempting to light a cigarette, he ignited gas escaping from an unlit blow pipe. He was entitled to benefit for the subsequent injury, for although he had converted a potential risk into an actual explosion, he had not made it a different danger or created a fresh danger.

An employee who suffers an accident, when acting in contravention of the law of his employer's orders, will nevertheless be entitled to injury benefit as long as two conditions are satisfied:

(*a*) The accident would have been deemed to have arisen out of and in the course of employment but for the prohibition, and
(*b*) The act was done for the purposes of, and in connection with the employer's trade or business (SSA section 52).

In one case an employee was injured whilst driving a fork lift truck. Although prohibited from driving the truck, he was nevertheless entitled to benefit, as he was acting within the scope of his employment in that he was using the truck to collect certain slings which he required for his work. In *R. v. Deputy Industrial Injuries Commissioner ex. p. Bresnahan,* a dock labourer engaged in loading a ship attempted to move pallets with a fork-lift truck. He was drowned when he drove the truck into the dock. His widow failed in her claim to obtain benefit, as he had no authority to drive the truck, and it was no part of his employment to move the pallets.

Intervals between periods of employment are normally covered by the Act e.g. tea breaks, smoking breaks, but if an employee exceeds the time allocated, he may well find that he is no longer entitled to benefit if an accident occurs during such an interval. In *R v. Industrial Injuries Commissioner ex.p. Amalgamated Engineering Union*, an employee overstayed his morning break of ten minutes by an additional five minutes when waiting outside a smoking booth for his turn to go in. While sitting outside the smoking booth he was injured by a fork-lift truck. It was held that in exceeding his permitted break he was no longer doing something reasonably incidental to his employment.

Different considerations apply to recreational activities. In *R v. National Insurance Commissioner ex.p. Michael* a police constable was injured when playing football for the force. It was held that although such an activity improved the morale and fitness of the force, it was nevertheless outside the formula. However, a fireman who was injured while performing in the brigade's agility team, used for publicity and recruiting purposes, was entitled to benefit as he was obliged to perform with the team as and when required.

Industrial diseases

An individual is entitled to benefit if he can show that he is suffering from one of the prescribed industrial diseases. It has long been recognised that certain diseases or injury are a hazard of certain occupations. There are some fifty-one diseases prescribed under the industrial injuries scheme, ranging from metal poisoning (lead, manganese, phosphorus etc) to anthrax, decompression sickness and tuberculosis. A recent addition to the list is occupational asthma.

The claimant must satisfy three conditions:

(*a*) He must be suffering from a prescribed disease, i.e. a disease listed in the Prescribed Diseases Regulations.

(*b*) This disease must be prescribed in relation to his occupation. Against the description of each prescribed disease, there is a list of the occupations for which that particular disease is prescribed e.g. anthrax – any occupation involving the handling of wool, hair bristles, hides or skins or other animal products or residues, or contact with animals infected with anthrax.

(*c*) The disease developed as a result of employment in that occupation, i.e. the claimant must establish a connection between the disease and the employment. There is a presumption that the disease is due to the nature of the occupation if the claimant has been employed in that occupation at any time up to one month of the onset of the disease. An insurance officer, seeking to rebut this presumption, must prove that on the balance of probabilities the disease did not occur as a result of the nature of the occupation.

There are three exceptions to this rule.
In the case of a claim for:

(*a*) *Tuberculosis* The claimant must have been first employed in the relevant occupation for at least six weeks, and have been last employed not more than two years before that date.

(*b*) *Occupational deafness*   He must have been employed for at least twenty years in a relevant occupation and must have been last employed not more than one year before the date of his claim.

(*c*) *Pneumoconiosis*   He must have been employed for two years in a relevant occupation.

If a claimant has been awarded benefit for one attack of a disease and then has a further attack, it will be necessary to determine whether he has contracted the disease afresh. If it is held to be a fresh attack, he will start a new disablement benefit period. If the attack is held to be a continuation of the first attack, i.e. a recrudescence, and this occurs within the disablement benefit period relating to the previous attack, it cannot provide the basis for a new claim, but it may be taken into account in reviewing a previous assessment of a claimant's disablement.

Disablement benefit

The Act provides for the payment of disablement benefit, payable for loss of physical or mental faculty as the result of an industrial accident or disease. Loss of physical or mental faculty is regarded as an impairment of the power to enjoy a normal life and is assessed by comparing the claimant's condition as a result of the accident with that of a normal healthy person of the same age and sex. It includes disfigurement even though this causes no bodily handicap.

The assessment is expressed as a percentage and is calculated by reference to a tariff set out in regulations. It ranges from 2 per cent for a 'guillotine amputation of a fingertip without loss of bone' to 100 per cent for loss of both hands and loss of sight 'to such an extent as to render the claimant unable to perform any work for which eyesight is essential'.

If the degree of disablement is assessed at less than 20 per cent, (e.g. loss of an index finger, 14 per cent) benefit will be paid as a gratuity. This is normally paid as a lump sum, but it may be paid in instalments to claimants under eighteen and to those individuals who request payment by instalments.

If the degree of disablement is assessed at 20 per cent or more, benefit will be paid as a weekly pension, as a lump sum payment cannot be awarded.

If the degree of disablement is assessed at 11 per cent or more and some other condition arises after the accident, but is not directly caused by it, the assessment will take cognizance of any increase in the degree of disablement as a result of that other cause.

The assessment does not take notice of any factors other than the physical or mental condition of the claimant. Disablement benefit is not affected by the nature of the claimant's employment or any loss of earnings power. It is payable irrespective of any earnings and whether the claimant has returned to work.

In certain cases disablement benefit is supplemented by other benefits. These further benefits endeavour to alleviate financial hardship resulting from the disability.

(*a*) A claimant may be entitled to *unemployability supplement* if, following the disablement, he is likely to be permanently unable to work or earn more than a limited amount in a year.

(*b*) If a claimant is so seriously handicapped as a result of the disablement (i.e. 100 per cent disablement) that he needs constant care and attention, he may be eligible for a *constant attendance allowance*.

(*c*) A *severe dsiablement allowance* is provided for those individuals who are so severely disabled, as a result of accident or injury, that they are in need of permanent attendance.

(*d*) A *hospital treatment allowance* is payable if an individual is an in-patient in hospital and receiving treatment for the injury for which the pension is payable. This allowance raises the disablement pensioner gratuity to the 100 per cent disablement rate.

(*e*) A *special hardship allowance* is payable if, because of the effects of disablement due to the accident or prescribed disease, the claimant is unable to return to his regular occupation or do work of an equivalent standard. The claimant must have a current disablement assessment of less than 100 per cent.

Death benefit

This benefit is payable, to a widow or other dependant, if the earner dies as a result of injury caused by an industrial accident or prescribed disease. If death is instantaneous the claimant must show that on the balance of probabilities the condition of the employment was the substantial cause of death, rather than a pre-existing condition. If death occurs after the accident, the claimant must show that on the balance of probabilities the industrial injury played a material part in bringing about the death. It need not, however, be the direct cause.

In one case an individual suffering from dermatitis (a prescribed disease) attended hospital for treatment of the disease. He later died after contracting pneumonia. It was held that the dermatitis had lowered his resistance to pneumonia, which he may have contracted as a result of stripping for various medical examinations in the course of the treatment for dermatitis.

The administration of the social security scheme

A claimant will initially present his claim for the appropriate benefit to an insurance officer at a local office of the Department of Health and Social Security. The insurance officer may allow the claim, refuse it, allow it in part, or refer the claim to the local appeal tribunal.

An appeal against the insurance officer's decision goes to a local appeal tribunal, which consists of an independent chairman and an equal number of members representing employers and employees. The local appeal tribunal also deals with claims referred to it directly by insurance officers. An appeal must be lodged within twenty-eight days of the date of the decision.

A further appeal may be made within three months (or longer period if the Commissioner so allows) to the Social Security Commissioner. An appeal may be lodged by an insurance officer, by the claimant or by any association which seeks to promote the interests and welfare of its members (e.g. a trade union) of which the claimant is, or was before his death, a member.

The appeal will normally be heard by the Chief Commissioner or one of the Deputy Commissioners. If the Chief Commissioner consider that an appeal raises a question of law of some complexity, he may convene a tribunal to consider the appeal consisting of himself and two Deputy Commissioners.

Certain questions arising from claims for benefit must be referred by the insurance officer either to the Secretary of State or to a local medical board for a decision. Medical question are decided by local medical tribunals who will determine the following questions:

(a) Whether the accident resulted in a loss of faculty for the claimant;

(b) If so, whether the loss of faculty is likely to be permanent;

(c) What is the degree of loss of faculty.

An appeal may be made from a decision of a local medical tribunal to a medical appeal tribunal. This consists of a chairman and two other members who are medical practitioners.

There is a further right of appeal, on a question of law, to the Social Security Commissioner. Leave to appeal must be obtained from the medical appeal tribunal or from the Commissioner.

There are certain questions that can only be determined by the Secretary of State. They include the following:

(a) Whether a person is an earner and, if so, in what category;

(b) Whether the contribution conditions for benefit have been satisfied;

(c) Which of two or more persons satisfying the conditions for an increase of benefit is entitled to the increase;

(d) Whether a person is or was employed in employed earner's employment for the purposes of benefit for industrial injuries and diseases.

A question of law arising in connection with any of the matters may be referred to the High Court by the Secretary of State, if he thinks fit. Any person who is aggrieved by the Secretary's decision in these matters may appeal from that decision, on a point of law, to the High Court. A decision may be reviewed by an insurance officer in certain circumstances:

(a) Where new facts have been brought to his notice; or

(b) He is satisfied that the decision was given in ignorance of some material fact; or

(c) The decision was based on a mistake as to some material fact; or

(d) There has been a relevant change of circumstances since the decision was given; or

(e) There has been a later decision of the Commissioner which undermines the basis of the previous decision.

Abbreviations

AC   Appeal Cases
A11ER   All England Reports
CA   Court of Appeal
Ch   Chancery
ICR   Industrial Courts Reports
IRLR   Industrial Relations Law Reports
KB   Kings Bench
KIR   Knights Industrial Reports
QB   Queens Bench
WLR   Weekly Law Reports

Appendix 1

Table of Cases

Page references are given in bold type

Appendix 2

The Employment Act 1982

Employee involvement

Section 1 requires directors' reports of larger companies to include a statement describing what action has been taken during the year to introduce, maintain or develop arrangements aimed at furthering employee involvement. It does so by amending section 16 of the Companies Act 1967.

New rights for those working closed shops

Section 2 enables the Secretary of State to pay compensation to many of the people who were dismissed without any remedy at the time because they were not union members in a closed shop between 1974 and 1980.

Sections 3 and 10 give new rights to individuals working in a closed shop not to be unfairly dismissed or have other action taken against them. It lays down three **additional** circumstances in which dismissal or action short of dismissal for non-membership of a trade union in a closed shop will infringe the employee's rights. These are:

1   Where a closed shop agreement has not in the preceding five years been approved in a secret ballot by 80% of the employees covered by it or by 85% of those voting;
2   Where at the time of dismissal the employee has obtained or is seeking a declaration from an industrial tribunal that he has been unreasonably excluded or expelled from the trade union to which he has to belong under the closed shop agreement; and
3   Where the employee is bound because of his qualifications to observe a written code of conduct and has left or been expelled from his union, or refused to join a union, because of a conflict between that code of conduct and a union instruction to take industrial action.

The first of these three extra safeguards will not take effect immediately. The Government's present intention is to bring it into force in two years so as to allow time for ballots to be held.

Section 3 also provides that an employee who cannot be fairly dismissed for non-membership of a trade union in a closed shop cannot be fairly dismissed either for refusing to make payments to the trade union or some other body or person in lieu of union membership.

Greater compensation for certain kinds of unfair dismissal

The act substantially increases the compensation for individuals found to have been unfairly dismissed either because of their trade union membership or activities or because of their non-membership of a union.

Section 4 introduces a minimum basic award of £2000 for anyone who is unfairly dismissed for one of these reasons.

Section 5 creates a new 'special award' of compensation payable in some cases to a person unfairly dismissed because of his trade union membership or activities or because of his non-membership of a union. The award is payable where the dismissed person asks an industrial tribunal to order his reinstatement or re-engagement, but no reinstatement or re-engagement results. In a case where the tribunal decides not to make an order for reinstatement or re-engagement, the amount of the award will normally be 104 weeks' pay, subject to a minimum of £10 000 and a maximum of £20 000. Where the tribunal makes an order, but the employer refuses to reinstate or re-engage in accordance with it, the amount of the special award will be 156 weeks' pay subject to a minimum of £15 000. In both cases the special award is additional to any basic or compensatory award. Both the special and the minimum basic award may be reduced on account of matters such as the employee's conduct before dismissal.

Section 6 ensures, however, that in these cases compensation will not be reduced merely because the person dismissed has broken a requirement in a contract or some other agreement that he must be a member of a union, or a requirement that he must not be a member of a union or take part in union activities.

Rights of 'joiner' extended

Sections 7 and 11 enable an employee who claims that he has been unfairly dismissed or had other action taken against him for not being a member of a trade union to request a tribunal to 'join' as a party to tribunal proceedings a trade union or other person that he claims put pressure on his employer to dismiss or take action against him by calling or threatening industrial action because he was not a union member. Where a trade union is 'joined' in the proceedings and the tribunal finds that it did exert such pressure on the employer, the tribunal can award compensation wholly or partly against the union rather than against the employer.

Right to apply for interim relief extended

Section 8 enables people who claim they have been unfairly dismissed for non-membership of a trade union to apply to a tribunal for an order of 'interim relief' (an order that their contract of employment should continue until their complaint of unfair dismissal is decided). People who claim to have been dismissed for trade union membership or activities can already apply.

Dismissal in connection with industrial action

Section 9 amends the law in this area. It provides that an employee who is dismissed while participating in a strike or other industrial action cannot claim unfair dismissal if the following conditions have been met:

1   His or her employer has dismissed all who were taking part in the action at the same establishment as the complainant at the date of his dismissal; and
2   His or her employer has not offered re-engagement to any of them within three months of their date of dismissal without making him a similar offer.

Protections for non-union companies

Sections 12 and 13 make void any term in a commercial contract which requires a person to use only union labour, or to recognise or negotiate with a trade union. They also make it unlawful to do any of the following simply because a company uses non-union labour, or does not recognise or negotiate with a union:

1   Exclude a company from a tender list;
2   Fail to permit a company to tender for a contract;
3   Fail to award a company a contract;
4   Terminate a contract with a company.

Section 14 makes unlawful any industrial action designed to put pressure on an employer to act contrary to the provisions described above. It also makes unlawful any industrial action which interferes with the supply of goods or services because:

1   Work done in connection with the supply of goods or services has been or is likely to be done by non-union members; or
2   The supplier of the goods or services in question does not recognise or negotiate with trade unions.

These provisions to protect non-union companies also protect unionised companies against discrimination because they *do* employ union members.

Trade union immunities

Section 15 abolishes the special immunities which have prevented trade unions from being sued in their own names. As a result it will become possible to sue a trade union for injunctions and damages if it authorises unlawful industrial action – such as industrial action outside a trade dispute, unlawful secondary action or secondary picketing. It will also become possible to sue a trade union if it is responsible for other unlawful acts whether or not connected with industrial action – such as defamation, trespass, negligence or nuisance.

Section 15 provides that a trade union is liable for unlawful industrial action organised by its officials if that action has been authorised or endorsed by:

1 Its Executive Committee; or
2 Its General Secretary or President; or
3 Any official who has authority under the union's own rules to call industrial action.

A union is also liable for unlawful action authorised or endorsed by its *employed* officials or any committees to which they report, unless:

1 The union rules prohibit the official or committee concerned from calling industrial action, or
2 The official or committee is overruled by the Executive Committee, President or General Secretary by means of a written 'repudiation' issued as quickly as is practicable, provided that the Executive Committee, General Secretary or President do not behave in a manner which is inconsistent with the repudiation.

Section 16 provides that where awards of damages are made against trade unions they will be subject to the following upper limits:

1 unions with fewer than 5000 members: £10 000
2 unions with between 5000 and 24 999 members: £50 000
3 unions with between 25 000 and 99 999 members: £125 000
4 unions with 100 000 or more members: £250 000

Section 17 protects certain trade union property from awards or damages, costs or expenses. These include personal property belonging to any trustee, member or official of the union concerned, and, in certain circumstances, property in a trade union's political fund or provident benefits fund.

Changes to the definition of a trade dispute

Section 18 amends the definition of a trade dispute, thereby redrawing the boundaries of lawful industrial action. These changes mean there will be a lawful trade dispute only when workers are in dispute with their own employer and the dispute is wholly or mainly about matters such as their pay, conditions or jobs. The changes will exclude from the definition of a trade dispute:

1 Disputes between a trade union and an employer who has no dispute with his own workers;

2 Disputes between trade unions or groups of workers where no employer is involved;
3 Disputes which are simply *connected* with pay, jobs etc rather than *wholly or mainly* about them; and
4 Disputes over matters overseas, unless the terms and conditions of those taking the industrial action are likely to be affected by the outcome of the dispute.

Law on 'sit-ins' clarified

Section 19 repeals section 13.2 of the 1974 Trade Union and Labour Relations Act, which had always been regarded as a declaratory provision providing no substantive immunity. Its repeal became necessary because of a court decision which suggested that it provided immunity for workers involved in 'sit-ins' and factory occupations.

Other provisions

The Act also makes some minor changes to various statutory employment protection rights and payments.

Index

COMPANY LAW

COLIN THOMAS

This comprehensive survey provides a clear introduction to the law as it relates to the formation, financing, control and winding up of companies in the UK, and particularly the provisions of the 1980 and 1981 Companies Acts and relevant case law.

The book looks first at the various types of companies and how they are incorporated, and at the memorandum and articles of association. It then examines the ways in which companies can be promoted and capital raised via shares, debentures and loans; the powers and duties of directors; and the role and responsibilities of the company secretary, accountant and auditor. The concluding chapters explore the legal complexities of liquidations, reconstructions, amalgamations and mergers, with reference to the City Code.

TEACH YOURSELF BOOKS